THE FEAST OF ICARUS

Memoir & Myth

THE FEAST OF ICARUS

Memoir & Myth

SAMUEL HAZO

Lambing Press, Pittsburgh.

To

Dr. Joseph C. Maroon

ICARVS ICARVS NOMINA DONAT AQVIS . SCIRE, DEI MVNVS, DIVINVM, EST NOSCERE VELLE. SED FAS LIMITIBVS SE TENVISSE SVIS. DVM SIBI QVISQ̊ SAPIT, NEC IVSTI EXAMINA CERNIT

To fly? No more a miracle than walking. Even doctors are perplexed by how our skin-sleeved and bone-buttressed shapes manage to be borne erect on our soles and heels and toes without collapsing into a mass, without tipping over or leaning left, right or forward, without, finally, so much as a passing thought of just how we do it. But we do it as did our predecessors and as will our successors. And no one marvels at this marvel. But talk or read of a man from Amsterdam or Washington who mimes the hawks, and our eyes enlarge, our lower jaws loosen a jot, and the questions start because we know as a matter of earthbound fact that man cannot fly. Only Icarus is exempt. Ask anyone to name the first man who flew, and the answer will, quickly or eventually, be the same. Icarus. No one seems to doubt that he swam the Mediterranean sky with his threatened and daring architect of a father from Crete toward Sicily. His tale is so much a part of us that we take the flight as fact. It's his flying too close to the sun that spawns the myth, that prompts our eyebrows to congeal and our hearts to pump, that stumps us with an ultimate why. We forget or ignore that the first myth is that he flew at all. Why isn't that enough for us? For centuries it hasn't been, and it isn't now. Not that he flew, no, that was not and is not what we see as his mission as well as his mistake, but that he flew too high.

The poet imitates Icarus. He is inspired to dare impossibility even if this means that he might and probably will fail in the attempt. His fate is to try to find silence's tongue, to say what is beyond saying, to mint from the air he breathes an alphabet that captivates like music. His victory, if it comes at all, must of necessity be a victory of the instant, a lyric split-second of triumph, quick as a kiss. He must live in, see through and simultaneously rise above. No wonder he has little in common with the historian or the philosopher, who tend to become soberer, even somberer, with age — as if the sheer weight of year after burdening year and the necessity of knowing and understanding and remembering were too much. But the poet concedes in advance to the years and all their baggage their ultimate pindown, their capacity to crush, their parenthesizing amens. Conceding this, he nonetheless wants to transcend the parentheses, as he must, en route. It was the poet in Icarus who dreamed of rising above a sealevel fate that would sadden and weigh him down long before it killed him. Feathering his arms, he flew into what couldn't be done. He knew impossibility would down him in the end, but up he went regardless. Why? For the poetry of it. Falling, he had the memory of a new height and no regrets.

Of his father, Daedalus, we know slightly more than the little we know of the son. An engineer he was in the fullest sense, the inventor of the hatchet, the carpenter's level and sails for ships, originally an Athenian before he decided to go to Crete to avoid retribution for his murder of Talos, a rather competitive nephew. Then came the unpleasant business with Minos, the king of Crete, who threatened to imprison him in the labyrinth which Daedalus himself had been commissioned to design and construct. Cornered, Daedalus conceived the idea of flying with Icarus to Sicily. So much for biography . . . I try to understand the man, father to father. I feel how he must have trained both himself and the boy to use the never-before-recycled feathers, how he must have wondered if the scheme would work and, if it did, how the two of them would be able to make it all the way to Sicily, a distance over unobligingly similar water of more than four hundred miles as the crow or the winged man flies. But suddenly I see him concluding that the feathers did indeed do what feathers were supposed to do, that the boy took to sky-swimming instantly, that he, the creator of the level and a man inured to the importance of balances, had to warn the boy to maintain a straight course at a fixed altitude in order not to jeopardize the fragile glue of the wing-wax. But the boy, as boys in the sky for the first time might be expected to do, refused to listen and decided to climb. I can almost hear the father scolding him in mid-air just before the first feather let go, then the second, then the third . . .

*F*oolhardy as it proved to be, the climb of Icarus certainly was not foolish in conception. After all, if one could fly at all, what was wrong with soaring? Icarus had no way of knowing in advance which altitudes were dangerous and which were not. He was simply yielding to the same urge athletes yield to when they raise the bar higher for one more jump, when they strain to hurl a javelin one inch farther than they've ever thrown it. So, whatever the urge was that inspired Icarus to ignore his father's advice and veer cloudward, sunward, starward, it was not out of the ordinary. And actually he was doing quite well until he ran afoul of the sun. Perhaps the sun, being the magnetic center of everything even though Icarus had no way of knowing that then, drew him higher or, rather, closer. Who knows? Summer moths flutter after the sunset around the sun's substitutes — lanterns, fires, incandescent bulbs — from a similar need. They are lured instinctively to illumination, the heated core of their brief universe. Icarus may have been obeying mere moth logic. Besides, who is able to resist a magnet when it means business? Part climb, part pull, the flight of Icarus was really a matter of the sun leashing him nearer and nearer until the wax thinned and ran and the feathers fell, and he plunged wingless into the waiting sea like a moth that has been singed into silence by the very fire that warmed it.

To say that Icarus simply dropped into the gulping sea, which was subsequently named after him, is not actually as I imagine it. Let me use a relatively recent incident to explain. Decades ago a ground-crewman was holding one of the mooring ropes of an American dirigible named the Akron when a quick windshift gusted the ship from its moorings. For some unknown reason the crewman held on to the mooring rope so that he rose with the ship — fifty feet, one hundred feet, two hundred and so up. In a matter of seconds he was as high as a skyscraper. Finally, he could no longer hold on to the rope, and he plummeted, kicking and flailing like a wild runner sprinting uselessly down the unsupporting sky. I see the fall of Icarus that way. It comes to me as a rebellion against space through space in space so that he did not slip without a splash into the stunning water but rather slammed into it, fighting gravity to the very end, straining so that the veins and cords in his forearms bulged as they do in the bronze casting of him made by the Bulgarian sculptor Valentine Starchev. Of course, the assumption is that Icarus drowned. But nothing exists to contradict my view that he survived. I see him surfacing after the plunge and then starting to swim surely to the nearest shore while his father, convinced now that the boy is all right, circles and hovers briefly before shouting down instructions and directions for a rendezvous. Years later, Daedalus builds a temple to Apollo at Cumae. My guess is that Icarus, having survived the fall and the long swim, probably helped him build it.

The sky begins at sea level, which means that all the space above the ground is someone's horizon, which means that air is our far and near and only element. What else is the earth but our foundation (and finally our covering when we pass out of the air) as we stand and walk headfirst into space? Perhaps this orientation not only confirms that we are creatures of the air but also explains why aviating attracts us more than spelunking, which is a sport without horizons. But whether we choose to roam caves or investigate and dive fathoms below the roof of the sea, we prove our dependence on the air by taking it with us in backpacks, in oxygen cylinders, in syringes, whatever. Actually more than our physical survival depends upon it. As long as we breathe, our imaginations breathe as well, which means we continue to create the dreams that we live in, on and invariably for and by. Dreams bloom in the aura of space that is the oxygen of the imagination. We feel that we have room and even that we are mysteriously elevated when our dreams begin to form and slowly realize themselves in what we make of them. And this applies to any kind of making from rising dough to the upward Gothic surge of the cathedral in Chartres to whatever Longinus meant when he equated sublimity with height. I see something of Icarus in all this, but I am tongue-tied to say what it is. If tulips or sunflowers could speak and describe whatever impels them to sprout and crane sunward for life itself, they would be able to say what I cannot say.

*I*t is nightfall in Antibes, and I am standing by the ramparts of the old city below the Picasso Museum on the eve of Bastille Day. It could be the eve of the Fourth of July in Chicago or Butte, but it is Antibes on Bastille Day minus one, and I am looking out through the darkness at three boats in an otherwise boatless harbor. I have been told that each of them is loaded with fireworks and that a spectacle is in the offing. Suddenly there is a rising hiss from the nearest boat, and I see something streak starward in a rush. For a second or more, silence. It is a macabre silence like a void before a thunderclap. Then there is a white burst a hundred feet or so over the boats, and I stare up at an enormous snowflake of fire that expands outward from the center of the burst and falls into the harbor like night snow. After that there is burst after burst, and the sky is crazy with flaming peonies, spider-webs of dazzling orange and pink, burning asterisks. Some of the bursts intersect simultaneously, and their showering designs collide like abstract paintings before they collapse together into the harbor. The exhibition continues for almost half an hour, and I turn to watch the faces of children who are seated on the rampart wall. The different explosions paint their faces with a rainbow of illuminations that Picasso would have memorized. Whenever they hear the rising hiss of a new rocket, the children watch expectantly but somewhat passively. It is the burst and fall that make their eyes glisten, and I imagine that my reaction must be similar. The climb of the varied explosions into the sky is a kind of preliminary prose to the poetry of the skyburst and skyfall. The ascent is what we barely see. We follow the rocket hiss with our ears. But the sundering at the peak of the climb and then the triumphant fall of so much color — that is what takes us.

Technically he was not the best of pilots, but Antoine de Saint-Exupery understood the air, and, when he wrote, he created a poetry of the air and of the men who sailed it in peace and war. Because he was an Icarus with more than a talent for flying, he could conjure with pen and paper a real sense of the sky, of men seated behind the earliest internal combustion engines as they crossed the Andes or the Sahara for the sake of delivering sacks of bundled letters, of goggled warriors who jockeyed in the clouds for gunsight views of one another. This imagery of the air permeated his style even when it was not the air that was his subject: "To prune the heart of man is not enough to save him; he must also be touched by grace. To prune the tree is not enough for it to bud; spring must also have a hand in the matter. To lighten the load is not enough for the plane to take off; a gust of wind from the sea is needed." Like all men whom systems cannot hold or satisfy, he constantly confronted himself with new challenges even when his age would have absolved him gracefully of the need. Who else but such a man could write: "But an administration is conceived as a safeguard against disturbances resulting from human initiative." Obedient finally to his own initiatives, which were the initiatives of one who understood the destiny of the artist as the man of action in our time, he flew his last mission in a plane appropriately called a Lightning. He died without a trace, but not before he had written: "Let a man in a garret but burn with enough intensity and he will set fire to the world." Saint-Ex's garret was a cockpit where, helmeted and goggled, he lived the life he wrote. It was his first address, and his last.

I know an architect who designed the tallest all-brick structure in the world. It is a twenty-two story apartment in Pittsburgh, Pennsylvania. When I told him I had seen brick buildings that were taller than his, he explained that there was a difference between brick buildings where the bricks simply covered a steel superstructure and brick buildings where there was no "steel skeleton" and where the bricks were doing "all the work." In his building, he stressed, the bricks were the primary source of support. I then asked him if twenty-two stories were the maximum height for such structures. His answer was that it was possible to go to forty-four. "Forty-five?" I asked. I was determined to learn the limit. He said that anything beyond forty-four would involve very careful calculations. Then he explained that the maximum height could never really be discovered since most architects as a matter of course as well as a matter of legal obligation kept their "artificial spaces" well below or within the maximum strengths of construction materials to allow for human miscalculation. This ended the conversation, but it left me unsatisfied. Yet, even allowing for human miscalculation, the entire problem struck me as having an Icarian dimension. How high was too high? How much was ever enough? Icarus "solved" the problem of finding his particular mean through experience. His excess preceded his fall, but somewhere in his excessive climb he passed where he should have stopped. But isn't this always the case? You either strike the exact balance (usually by luck) or you go beyond it. Undershooting is no help; that still leaves the mean unknown. Overshooting reveals it by passing it. So Blake was right when he said, "You never know what is enough unless you know what is more than enough."

I often wonder what the twentieth century will be remembered for. Its wars and its war-dead? I doubt it. Who recalls with precision the slaughters and casualties of the Crusades or the multitudinous pillages of Genghis Khan? There seems to be something about the memory of the race (and individual memory as well) which blots out the horrible, which suppresses it, which wants not to recall. Or will the century be remembered as the one which saw infantile paralysis vanquished by vaccine or as the time when human hearts were transplanted from chest to chest? Possibly. But my suspicion is that our best legacy will be the astonishing progress in aviation from the eighteen-second flight of the Wright brothers to intercontinental jet travel and interplanetary rocket exploration today. To me this is as indelible an address in history as the industrial revolution was in the nineteenth century. And like the industrial revolution it is beyond repeal. It permanently influences our lives just as the industrial revolution did and does. In the latter case no less a spokesman than Frank Lloyd Wright stated that it meant the end of the world's great cities. Citing Paris and Rome and Vienna as true cities, Wright noted that their pre-industrial genesis meant that factories could not be built in them but outside them. In post-industrial cities the reverse is true and probably will remain true. Analogically, the capability of moving from hemisphere to hemisphere by air in a matter of hours has transformed our ideas about locomotion. Space is reduced to time whenever we ask how long it will take us to fly from one point to another. Not how far but how long! We think less and less in miles and more and more in minutes. And since each scientific advancement in aviation is usually an advancement in the speed of aircraft, it is possible to say that aviation in its own way is an attempt to approach the speed of thought itself. In our century, therefore, we have gone beyond the dream of Icarus and the aeronautical drawings of Leonardo da Vinci and the Mayan carvings of their winged progenitors. We have tried and will continue to try to move closer to instantaneity, which is where the mind always flies.

*M*oving up! How many times have I heard that phrase as if it were the one and only synonym for progress or growth. There is something of the myth of Icarus in this inasmuch as it is assumed that the greater the height the greater the achievement and concomitant peril — as if individual and social life were built on the principle of ascension. Corporate tables of organization, for example, are established to be read from the top down so that the lower echelons are encouraged to dream of rising in the corporation. Office managers often refer like sergeants or colonels to the people "under them." And such bourgeois imagery as the "ladder of success" or "rising like cream to the top" or "becoming number one" or "standing head and shoulders over everybody else" merely enforces this hierarchy of ascent. Nor is this simply confined to the bourgeoisie. What of the long-standing tradition equating competence or excellence with the reward of "elevation," as is common in politics, academic life and the church? This is to say nothing of the tendency of believers to "look up" to God on the assumption that the divinity and the afterlife are somehow an overlife, that heaven is up and hell is down and so forth. What is at the heart of all this? Is it the desire to get away from the earth, to shuck gravity, to give oneself to the idea that up is freer than down? Regardless, it is certainly contrary to that inwardness and divine abandonment that distinguish the sufi and the saint and all truly humble men and women. But even here the desire to ascend is present. Just think of those who took to the tops of mountains to flee with God, to retreat for perspective, to receive the Commandments, to scale like Hart Crane the royal palm of poetry. These people did not go into caves. They went to Sion, to Olympus, to the Mount of Olives, to the Himalayas. Always up, up, up. Why?

laustrophobia and the fear of suffocation are twins. Most of us would readily admit that we usually try to avoid circumstances which might place us at the mercy of either. Which suggests to me that we are ordinarily attracted to their exact opposites — spaciousness and oxygen. I would go further and say that these two elements find their perfect synthesis in flight, which is essentially a matter of navigating the very air we breathe. Who has not felt a vicarious rise in his spirit when he watches a chickenhawk coast the high winds over a mint field? And what is it that makes the eyes of boys shine when their kites catch the right currents and climb as far as their fishing strings permit, becoming like manta rays fighting to escape the lines and fastenings that will finally tug them home. And I could say the same for hang-gliding and everything else that qualifies as heavier-than-air-flight. It's as if spaciousness and the open air offer us life without the usual limitations, and such a concept of life attracts us. It appeals to those of us who agree with William James' observation that too many people live within limitations that are not only self-imposed but well below the limits of real challenge. Such people are not Icaruses. Icarus stands for a life that wants to exceed its limits, that wants to make its only horizon what it's yet to see or do, that hungers to carry possibility to a point where possibility and impossibility blur. That this tests the human spirit is obvious. That its acceptance requires valor is also obvious, particularly in those instances when one must proceed without knowing in advance where the final limits are and where no precedent exists to offer even the flimsiest guidance.

The first time I saw the Winged Victory of Samothrace, I had the impression that the entire Louvre must have been built around it. It dominated the landing on which it was centered as totally and majestically as the statue of the resurrected Christ dominates high Corcovado above Rio de Janeiro. When I walked up the museum stairs and looked at the flexed and fractured wings of the statue, I knew all at once why victory is always a winged thing. Granted, man learns a great deal about his real stature in defeat, which induces its own ruthless honesty and self-examination. But in victory he knows what uplifts, and the Winged Victory or the Nike of Samothrace is the prime symbol of that. In defeat a man has to struggle not to look earthward. In victory his spirit burns in his eyes, and his eyes regard everything from those inner altitudes which luck or endurance or sheer effort has gained for him. The cage of his limitations is shattered by his vision, and for a moment he knows what heroes alone know. There is a German idiomatic phrase in which the worst kind of defeat is described as happening when one is destroyed on the ground. Apart from the militaristic and aeronautical implications of the phrase, it has always suggested to me the helplessness of not being able to rise. But victories of almost every kind are invariably associated with ascent — scaling a peak, finishing on one's feet, gaining the higher score, jumping to new heights, finishing on top and on and on. In all of these instances it is easy to hear the quiet flexing of the wings of the Nike. There is no such thing as a winged defeat.

If Icarus fell because he ignored a simple law of physics, it is possible to see in his saga not merely man's constant inclination to test the frontiers of possibility but also the darker impulse to exceed or violate other laws. It probably never occurred to Icarus that the sun would undo him simply because it was the sun; he thought he would not be affected. Similarly, to be "above the law" suggests to some people that the law does not refer to them, and this could apply to everything from local and national statutes to natural law as well. Such people live in the false altitudes of superiority. This may have been partly involved in the act of Cain when he "rose up" against his brother. It may be what often transforms a sense of authority into the arrogance of power. Isn't power itself associated with superiority, with overloading, with dominance, with being above rather than beneath? And this same heady air could be what lures the gambler back for one more "trick" in the belief that he will recoup all his losses and then some. In each of these instances there is the unmistakable strain of non-acceptance, which is the primal mark of Icarus in our nature, but, as all the Cains and Caesars of history attest, it is possible to be a non-accepter for the worst as well as for the best of reasons.

For the sick, non-acceptance of their sickness is frequently synony-mous with life — not life as it is for them in their sickness but life as it used to be for them or as they would like it to be again. I saw this in the most heart-cutting way when my father at eighty-two suffered a stroke. An active man all his life, he was suddenly forced to adjust to spending day after day in bed or propped against pillows in a chair. The stroke was of the type that paralyzed his right side and left him with a slight slur in his speech, but his mind was unimpaired. From May when the stroke felled him until mid-August when a second stroke killed him, he struggled daily to walk and to will his right hand back into use. He had no patience with doctors or nurses who attempted to make him relax and adjust and more or less resign himself. One doctor told me candidly on more than one oc-casion, "Your father simply will not accept his condition." By the tone of the doctor's remarks I found myself influenced, perhaps even recruited, to convince my father to accept what the doctors believed he should accept. On numerous occasions I explained that he would have to make the best of things with what the stroke had not touched, that we would always be near him, that there was still a lot to live for and even more to do. I became a veritable priest of platitudes. My father just looked at me, never agreeing and never really disagreeing overtly, but he kept on trying, trying, trying to force his dead right side to come alive again. It was not until after he died that I realized that all my counsels about acceptance were like a sentence of death to him. His very resistance to me and to the doctors was proof to him that he was still his own man, not ours. As a result, his refusal to accept his incapacity became the very motivation for his vain efforts to try to make his right hand and right leg obey him again. Acceptance would have forced him to abandon the effort, and that would have killed him days and weeks before he actually died. It was the struggle that mattered, and to him that was all that mattered. In retrospect all his seeming stubbornness in the face of my "advice" and the all-too-clinical correctness of the doctors only makes me admire and love him more now.

*I*carus could easily be the god of fountains. The beautiful but ultimately futile and purposeless ascent of water from some upthrusting spring always reminds me of him. There is the same war against gravity, the same climb from high to higher to highest, the same tension in the ascent and the same listless grace in the descent. I remember, for example, watching for as long as half an hour the jet d'eau in Geneva. I stared as the waterjet worked its way up from a small, frothy upheaval to a spray-fringed pillar of white water. The core of the pillar kept nosing upward, peaking as it rose and spraying the lake and lakeshore below with shower after wind-curled shower. It mesmerized me as moving water (or fire) has always mesmerized me. Water-dance. Fire-dance. Each of the two elements keeps creating itself in its own constantly original way. With fire it is always a sequence of flashing and vanishing until the last sizzle. But with fountaining water it is a liquid ballet. The grace is a grace that only water on the rise can create. First, the powerful push to the sun. Then the powerless fall from the highest point of the push. In Geneva I watched the pure energy of water as it speared up from its spring, and I had the impression that, like a rocket to the moon, it could go wherever it wanted. But the farther it soared from the earth, the weaker the jet grew until it seemed to pivot on the height of its own strength before it plunged back with a spent, shattered diminuendo that proclaimed the earth had won again. When it rose, the water was concentrated like a stalk. But in the fall the stalk flared open and down like willow branches sleeved with melting snow.

*T*hat we live within restraints is true. That we would like to live without restraints is also true. I am not thinking of people like Coleridge who wanted to escape all the restrictions of British institutionalism and live unfettered on the banks of the Susquehanna. (Why the Susquehanna? Simply because Coleridge liked the sound of the name.) Nor am I thinking of rebellion against oppression or the lure of nudism, which tends to be a warm-weather credo at best. The problem is more subtle than that. What I have in mind are those times when we overstep ourselves without fully understanding how or why what is happening is happening. When, for example, does casual bantering suddenly become anger? When does a passing attraction become the desire to possess? When does dining to satiety become gluttony? If I asked how instead of when, I am sure the answers to these questions would remain just as elusive. In the history of every person there are instances when he or she no longer tolerated a restraint, resisted what confined or limited, broke through if only to discover that more restraints like more horizons were created by the effort. The restraint could have been anything from a speed limit to the dictates of fashion. Or it could have been reason itself. The impulse to go beyond reason and even to want to live beyond reason is as old as Icarus. Older, in fact. It is as if the promise of life lies not within bounds but beyond bounds, and it is the rare man or woman who has not responded to the summons of that promise for selfish or for the most noble reasons. The passion of Caligula to concentrate in his own person the infinite possibilities of power is an example of the former. As for the latter, I think of what the widowed Ruth in the Old Testament said to her mother-in-law Naomi after Naomi urged her to do the sensible, the reasonable, the natural thing and marry again: "Whithersoever thou shalt go, I will go: and where thou shalt dwell, I also will dwell. Thy people shall be my people, and thy God my God."

The fact that Daedalus was an engineer undoubtedly helped him to conceive the idea of escaping by air from Crete. But once he and Icarus had glued feathers to their arms with wax, they stood and flew as equals. I mean they were equal in the sense that they were the first winged men in history. The key difference between them as flyers was simply that one was older than the other. Their teacher was the sky itself, and as students of the sky they learned as they went. Anyone who has ever worked with students can easily see how similar the life of learning is to the flight of Daedalus and Icarus. In the pursuit of truth the only teacher is the subject being studied. The pursuers are all students, some younger, others older. Young minds are just as capable of discovery and insight as older minds, and the prudences of age are readily counter-balanced by the impatience of youth. Rebuked because of their youth and inexperience, the young might easily repeat what Haimon says to Creon in the *Antigone* of Sophocles: "But if I am young and right, what difference does it make if I am young?" Ignored because they are older, the elderly might change the adjective in Haimon's statement and make the same point. For years I've worked as an annually eldering student among students who annually stay the same age. By introducing them to poems I feel something of what Daedalus must have felt when he saw Icarus take off into the risky, alluring sky toward Sicily. I have seen the foreheads of students congeal with the pain of understanding thoughts in collision, have come away frequently frustrated with my inability to say exactly what I meant, have fought to stay clear of the sloughs of pedantry. It took years for me to accept the simple fact that everything a man knows is not as important as how he thinks and feels and sees. It took more years for me to realize that learning how to let students think with you while you simultaneously think with them is where and how minds take fire. The consequences of such co-thinking are impossible to predict, and this is as it should be. In this context I remember two of my own teachers. One had the Socratic ability of stimulating more questions than answers. Indeed, he seemed suspicious of answers, especially dogmatic answers. His genius as a teacher was that he could touch the minds of his students and set them in motion until they slowly got the hang of the intellectual life. Once he said that the role of the teacher was to lead his students into the jungle and let them find their own way out. The second teacher was a swimming instructor. He had the gift of compelling beginners to face their own fear of water and then learn their way out of it. He would corner them with challenges in deep water where swimming was the only solution. From the time he was in his twenties until he retired well into his sixties, he had the vocation of seeing to it that no one who left his classes did so without knowing how to swim, which is not a bad legacy. How many lives did he save? How many souls?

omance and Icarus? Hardly synonymous in the minds of lovers or scholars, but there is a connection. What is it that lovers enjoy most but the elation of their own condition, and what do they enjoy more but the heightening of that elation? For the incurable romantic the principal value in his or her life is that renewal or repetition of the experience of "being in love," which is not the same as loving, by any means. Romantic lovers everywhere are studies in levitation, proving again that Mercutio was nothing but erotically correct when he told Romeo that "a lover may bestride the gossamer that idles on the wanton summer air and yet not fall, so light in vanity." Vanity is the air in every lover's balloon. It suspends him, carries him on and on, lifts and wafts him on the winds of his own illusions. The more adventuresome or exciting or dangerous the risks taken in the name of love, the greater the exhilaration of the experience and the stronger the temptation to repeat the experience for an even greater exhilaration. Vanity thus becomes not only a lighter-than-air gas but is even lighter than breath, than life itself. Witness Don Juan. He loved once, repeatedly. But the sincere are no more immune than the lecherous from being attracted to forbidden dalliances. The ability of the merely diversionary to uplift before it lets down is too common an experience to be doubted, let alone denied. And what seduces the temptee may be as common as boredom or as invitingly vivid as Simenon's desire to play with "a new pair of breasts." Usually a single venture into more dangerous or at least different air is not sufficient. Further sallies are almost inevitable as corroborated by the Frenchman who said that he knew "many women who never had a single affair but he knew none who had only one" and as further proved by Napoleon Bonaparte's preferences for Caroline Colombier, Desiree Clary, Josephine Beauharnais, Marguerite Pauline Foures, Madames Grassini and Georges, Marie Walewska and assorted unknowns.

*S*uppression creates resistance. And active resistance against intolera-
ble suppression always summons us to rely on the verbs of ascension
to characterize it. Rebellions are thus called uprisings. Guerrillas mount
attacks against their adversaries. For the rebel, being indomitable means
finally not being put down. And rebels and revolutionaries do not rest until
they have gained the upper hand. The final victory means the lowering of
one flag and the hoisting up of another. Height rhymes with the atmosphere
of supremacy and is the antithesis of all that is down trodden. All this is
familiar, even platitudinous, but what is at the basis of this resistance, this
unwillingness to acquiesce to subjugation, this arterial no? Politically, there
are many reasons, but what is common to all is that resistance, or rather the
courage to resist, is the child of hatred and fear. It is fear that first fires the
rebel-to-be, fear of his oppressor, for himself and those dear to him. This
then is replaced by hatred for the individual or group or nation that is the
cause of this fear. The two feelings co-exist for a time until the rebel-to-be
reaches a point where he begins to hate what he fears more than he fears
it. At that instant he becomes a resister and proceeds to find the means to
implement his will to resist. Frequently such sagas end in the overthrow of
oppressors and are just as frequently followed by excesses of "justice" on the
part of the overthrowers. It is inevitable. Hold dry wood under water for a
time and then release it quickly, and the wood will rise to the surface with
such force that it will go higher than the surface itself before it settles on
the sea.

spiration? Like inspiration its root is in the Latin verb for breathing. Like inspiration, aspiration touches on the fact that what relates to life relates to breath and conversely. Despite this, aspiration has come to mean more than merely breathing upon, which is its literal definition. An aspirant has come to mean someone who wishes to climb. A candidate aspires. An athlete aspires. And by the same logic I find it poetically possible to say that tulips aspire, that skyscrapers aspire, that a spire aspires. Regardless of poetic license, there is no doubt that aspiration seems to identify height with achievement or fulfillment. Perhaps the desire for gaining perspective proceeds from this same spring. At the top of his imagined birch Robert Frost concluded that the earth was the right place for love, but he could not find it in himself to say so until he saw the earth from a given height. True, an aspirant is usually someone whose desire to climb is prompted by a certain ambition, but it is clearly possible to be as ambitious for perspective, which is more than what is corporately called an "overview," as it is for fame or power. The humanist, for instance, can hunger to "see life steadily and see it whole" with the same intensity that inflames the eyes of all the marathoners who annually run for the Boston prize. No one, I suspect, aspires to die. But, in one sense, how can death be excluded? Death in its deepest mystery makes possible the final elevation since it realizes the ultimate victory of space over time whereby the dead are translated, as those left alive can testify, from somewhere at some time to everywhere all the time.

Icarus poisons our ease. Why fly? Why not dream the lotus lander's dream where pears swing green and plump and not too high, where brooks can chill as many flagons of the purest burgundy that any vintner can bottle, where sea and sand and wind are all the ambience that exists as far and long as we can breathe? If wonder is the brain's bread, what man can starve as long as there are stars and eagles and the matching silkscreen wings of all the moths they call sequopia? Why fly then, why think of it, why fret? Better, we say, the slow slide that says we will not fatten if we gorge, not slice the loyal heart if we turn goatish on a whim and not, not, not be drawn and quartered by the nervous king whose kingdom is our very skulls where he rules and waits for nothing but our dalliance to let him speak in the most precise commandments. Even as we sink we want to hear only the other voice that says we need our rest, that we deserve it now and after now and after that, that we have had enough of having the worst happen after the worst was supposed to be past forever. Better, we say, the self-reprieve where nothing, really nothing happens, good or bad, and we can float unsleeping on the earth's so slowly counterclocking course and know without a word the silent pulse of rocks. Why not? But somewhere at the bottom of our dreams a boy with wings is paying no attention to us, none at all. He smiles and lets us talk. When we are still, he smiles away our reasons and our protests and our arguments like so many mirages, and then he orders us to follow him. He says the sky is waiting.

*L*indbergh in prospect is not the same as Lindbergh in retrospect. In retrospect he is Paris and praise and a ride through tickertape s n o w in New York and, afterward, the matter of a son kidnapped and killed and then the flap with Roosevelt and then the war and finally the last flight to an island grave in Hawaii. In prospect he is different. He is seated in the Spirit of St. Louis. It is raining lightly, and he is just lifting off from an airfield on Long Island, just clearing the surprisingly high telephone wires at the end of the field and wondering if he has not weighted the plane with too much gasoline, just veering slightly north toward Nova Scotia and Newfoundland in the first landhugging arc before he dares the Atlantic. The biggest problem is sleep, or rather the lack of it. He's been too excited and occupied to sleep, and he now faces thirty to forty hours when sleep will be fatal. Was it lack of sleep that doomed the others: Nungesser, Davis, Wooster, Coli, Byrd, Bennet, Novile and Fokker? Or was it bad luck or flaws in the equipment or-or-or? He speaks to the Spirit of St. Louis as to a good wife, modulating the gasoline flow as he speaks so that the consumption from separate tanks will be as equal as possible in order to avoid any yaws or lists. He forgets his sandwiches completely. The deaths of all the other pilots from both continents are already a history of defeat after defeat, and it stays with him. History insists that what he's doing can't be done, but still he does it, is doing it, and history is listening or rather history is happening with the passage of one ocean mile after another beneath the shadow of his wings. To keep awake he tells himself that there is "no alternative but death or failure," and only his fear of one or the other or both shocks him back from sleep. Ahead of him now is death or Ireland. After he passes Ireland, it becomes death or Paris. Even though he believes that he has enough fuel left to reach Rome, he tells himself that he might be wrong. After all, the purpose was to cross the "3,600 statute miles" of the Atlantic, wasn't it? Why risk a crash in the Alps? But still, but still . . .

*B*egin with pipesmoke. It writhes upward from the burl bowl like a vaporous cobra charmed out of its jar. It changes, doubles, flattens, goes vaguely cloudy and dissipates. Likewise with leafsmoke. From a slow smolder it escapes from the heaped mulch in wisps exactly as campfire smoke exits from the gap in the capping flaps of a wigwam. And, of course, do not forget incense. What is the very purpose of incense but to rise from swung or swinging censers and float like dissolving smoke-rings into the arched ceilings of cathedrals? The locomotives of another decade would spew from their stacks a streamlined funnel of coal smoke, and the smoke in turn would scarf the entire length of the train and then remain momentarily suspended after the caboose finally passed under it. It seemed like a wake in mid-air before it rose into the sky and vanished along with the receding kudda-hum-kudda-hum-kudda-hum-ha-roo of the already out-of-sight locomotive in much the same way as a ship's wake softens from the first sudsy white churnings into a slowly widening wedge that follows the ship like a great arrow before it smooths out and returns to the will of the sea once more. What were the smoke signals of the Sioux and the Comanches but messages without a memory. No sooner were they seen and read than they erased themselves. Or seemed to erase themselves. It was really all a matter of the smoke becoming sky again. It is the first law of smoke, and the last and only. The higher the smoke goes, the sooner does it dissolve. Dissolved or subsumed, it is no longer what it was. To be smoke it must ascend. But when it ascends it does so only at the cost of no longer remaining smoke. Yet it must ascend.

THE FEAST OF ICARUS

I call it Saturday soup because I make it on winter Saturdays. The ingredients are whatever is at hand. Into boiling water I feed beef bones and beef chunks and then wait as the fat and dross come to the surface as a foaming malt-like scum that I skim with a perforated spoon. Then come salt, pepper, garlic, many onions sliced like silver dollars that will gradually boil into slivers, some powdered beef stock or bouillon cubes and one bay leaf. After half an hour I add whole stewed tomatoes and then walk away and smoke an unhurried cigar while everything in the pot bubbles on and becomes more or less intimate. After two hours I sluice in potatoes cut to the size of sugar cubes, carrot nickels and dimes, enough sliced peppers to establish a presence, another spray of salt and garlic, celery leaves and possibly some diced escarole or cabbage depending on availability and the way I happen to feel about escarole or cabbage on that particular Saturday. Everything in the pot has now been tumbling together so that one flavor has blended with another, and the soup is starting to look like soup. Now is the time to leave well enough alone and let the ingredients do all the work. I watch the jumble and tumble of potatoes and carrots and beef and onion as each somersaults its way to the top of the pot before disappearing into the depths again. Just then I pour two cups of lentils or barley or pastina and watch the smaller grains join the boiling salad that keeps rising and falling within itself like a submerged Ferris Wheel. At this time I invariably think of Willa Carter's comment that the same impulse is behind the making of a cake as is behind the invention of a poem. My soup mixes the metaphor a fraction or two, but its genesis and growth into its final cornucopia have something of the mystery of the making of a poem about them. You start with a whim for what will happen when you put bone, beef, and a scrambled alphabet of herbs and vegetables into a cauldron and then let them grope toward flavor just as a poem seethes and flounders toward its meaning. Icarus would understand since all making is like a flight into skies that the flyer reads as he goes. There are no real blueprints, just guesses. My soup is what it turns out to be. No revisions.

The second of the thus far two world wars saw the widespread use of floating airports for military purposes. Prosaically but functionally christened aircraft carriers, they roamed the oceans, predominantly though not exclusively the Pacific, whose peace-denoting name is a further irony for those with an ear for what is linguistically unsuited to its essence. "Flat-tops" later emerged as a more poetic designation than aircraft carriers, but in fact the flat tops merely described the decks of these enormous ships. In below-deck hangars were stored squadrons, and in addition to pilots these ships carried hundreds of sailors with specialties in everything from cooking to firefighting. Because these carriers were themselves vulnerable to attack from the air as well as from sub-surface and surface ships, they were usually accompanied in cordon by destroyers, cruisers and battleships. Launched from their often pitching decks, the carriers' fighters and dive-bombers would form squadrons in the upper air and streak to their missions and then return to land on the same decks from which they had been launched earlier. The landing of crippled aircraft was an experience in peril, and there is documentary footage that graphically shows planes exploding into flames as they crash into conning towers, planes overshooting and vaulting into the sea, planes missing the deck entirely and crushing anti-aircraft gunners, planes nosing over as the restraining rows of deck cables miss and miss the fuselage hook and then finally catch. More poignant to me than these homing disasters are those stories of pilots returning from their missions to find no carrier at all waiting for them. Unaware that the carrier had been sunk during their absence, the pilots would be condemned to search and search the endless darkening meadows of the sea for their only hope. With one eye on their gasoline gauges and another on the clueless ocean, they would fly and fly, breaking radio silence only to be answered by silence. I imagine these doomed pilots at that last instant when the fuel needle touches empty and below empty, which is as valid an equivalent as the earliest aviator's watching the sun melt the wax from his feather-woven wings. I think of each of those new Icaruses as their motors begin to miss and sputter. They try the radio one last time. Perhaps they bail out at this point, but I suspect that they remain in the cockpit as if reluctant to leave the plane's womb. When the propellers stop for the last time, they ride their planes into the sea that receives them like the waiting grave it always was and is and shall be.

ithin whatever future we imagine we have left (or have coming to us) we presume to live. Even though we know that life's permanent address is the present tense, we cannot live in that present without the hope, however vague (indeed, preferably vague), that this present will be succeeded by a subsequent present and then another and another and another. It is the possibility of a future, which for us means a present to come, that permits our present lives to continue to happen, but for such happening to happen it is essential that this future be indefinite. Knowing, for instance, that we have exactly five hours or five weeks or five years to live immediately turns us into the condemned. Our blood becomes poisoned with exactitude, and we are left to fret on the cross of our sentence. But as long as we do not know the terms of our sentence, we live in the pretense that the date of our execution is, at any rate, not immediate. We continue to create horizons for ourselves since not knowing what is to come and when it is to come is both a reprieve and an incentive. As long as we voyage in these spaces, we are doing nothing more than living as men live. But too often our restlessness and our curiosity make this condition seem insufficient. We hunger to know more about what is actually unknowable. How severe a winter will we have? How intelligent and happy will our children be? Will the plane in which we are being flown land safely? Will the horse on which we have gambled our savings win the race of races? Will we be spared cancer? To arrive at answers to these unanswerables we take instruction from the stars, the spent leaves of tea in a cup, the intersecting rivers of creases in the human palm, the transparent globes of soothsayers, the kingdom of dreams or the dicey sorcery of a pack of playing cards. Or else we take the future into our own hands and pronounce without hope of refutation that what we expect to be true will be true because we expect it. This man will lose the election, that attack will fail, this song will never be popular, that effort will be in vain, this daughter will resemble her mother, that unborn child will be a boy. The illusory certitude of our prescience imbues us with infallibility — an infallibility that only the yet-to-be can refute or confirm. The result is that our very conclusiveness stops our need to think further, and we relax with our prognostication like a squirrel with its nut. But even as we relax, why is it that such foretellings leave us uneasy? Is it fear that we might be wrong? Is it that we have, like the ancient Greeks, tempted the gods with our excesses, our presumptions, our arrogant omniscience? Or is it simply that, by making the unknown conform to our profile of how it will come to be, we close the minds (and thus our lives) — to wonder?

*W*hen Icarus first took to his wings, he had to concentrate carefully on what he was doing, which was, after all, soloing on his first flight. He had to flap his wings in unison and keep his body as level in the air as a swimmer must on the surface of the water. He could not think of failure or success. He could not worry about gauging his speed. He could not glide and appreciate the view. Perhaps as his flight progressed, he might have indulged in such thoughts and acts as he learned to move his arms less self-consciously and more automatically, but in the beginning he had to think only and exactly of what had to be done and then he had to will his body into doing it. And it is how he acted in the beginning that interests me since it was at this point that his mind and body were most loosely synchronized. It was then that he was most conscious of himself or rather abreast of himself second by second. Conscious action is best defined as what happens when man is most aware of himself and knows it. What he is doing at that moment occupies him totally, animates him totally, draws him on totally. It happens both by premeditation and by talent and by accident as when a speaker finds himself saying precisely what he means, achieving in ways that he cannot fully explain the sudden inspiration of felt speech. It happens when a kiss is given with the focus of the whole person behind it, when a vaulter launches himself up and over the bar in the most perfect way of which he is capable, when a surgeon's fingers move with a purpose and skill that transcend habit and training, when a child walks for the first time or when any writer knows and feels that he is weaving out his meaning as he goes, discovering it and writing it simultaneously, never going beyond himself because there is no beyond to go beyond. It is all now. It is all here.

Because Minos was determined to jail or possibly kill him if he remained, Daedalus chose to escape from Crete. Like most escapes, his was prompted by a desperation born of necessity. In this case, necessity started the pearl of invention to grow like an embryo in the engineer's mind, and the result was that Daedalus created a place for himself in the mythology of the world. Departures are one thing, but departures without the possibility of return are another. Consider Daedalus' options. On one hand, prison and death. On the other, a mode of travel that was, to say the least, probably undreamed of and certainly untested. Once airborne, he simply had to continue. No maps. No chance to rest en route. No room for mistakes. Daedalus thus emerged as the prototypical immigrant as well as a pioneer, and he was both simultaneously. Think for a moment of subsequent immigration — one-way immigration. Think, for example, of the thousands upon thousands who came to the United States from Europe in the first decade of the twentieth century. Like Daedalus, they knew — most of them knew that they were leaving their homelands for the last time as well as the first time, and thus the only time. Ahead was the unknown country of total risk and total promise. The courage that was and is required for such journeys is the stuff of which sagas are made. It leaves almost no room for error, and one's whole life is the wager. The immigrants' reasons for leaving one hemisphere and coming to another were variants on the theme of Daedalus. Flight from political oppression, economic slavery, poverty, hopelessness, want . . . The America they sailed for was already in their hearts and heads. As a promise, a beckoning, a beginning, it was growing pearl-like within them as they crossed the Atlantic. Already they were creating it so that their subsequent lives often resembled for them the living out of a dream. So, they shared the challenge of Daedalus, and they knew something of the threat that made it possible and inevitable. And after they landed in their new world they remembered the whole epic of the crossing from one life to another, as Daedalus must have after he reached Sicily, with a kind of disbelief and wonder.

*N*ot the light in the eyes of Romeo when he first glimpsed Juliet in profile nor the new life in Dante's eyes at the sight — his only sight — of Beatrice. Not the look of Monica when she saw Augustine at his worst. Not the slow, still disbelieving stare of Orpheus when he dropped his lyre and saw, at that instant, Eurydice, alive again. Not the blurred softness in the eyes when tears are their final and only possible words as when lovers meet after long separations or know they will never meet again. These are not the eyes of Icarus. Rather the straight gaze of fisherman who spend long periods at helms reading the fish-thick prairies of the Baltic or El mar Caribe. Or the crow-footed squint of cowboys and hunters. Or the measuring looks of bakers as they bake. Or the quickness in the eyes of athletes, especially baseball players at bat with the ball coming. Or the eyes of operators in control towers monitoring radar. Or the eyes of surgeons in the very act of surgery. Or the eyes of poets when a poem starts and they go with it. Or the eyes of seamstresses. Or the eyes of grooms and brides or all those who choose someone else irrevocably. Or the eyes of women in the final weeks and even hours of pregnancy. Hemingway's eyes. The eyes of Albert Camus. The eyes of pilots as they land compared to the eyes of those on the ground who watch them land. Picasso's eyes. The eyes of a medieval monk of Bulgaria who carved scenes from the life of Christ in a rosewood diptych the size of a dinner platter in ultra-microscopic detail over a period of a decade, carving every day as long as the light lasted, losing his sight completely on the day the work was finished. The monk is anonymous, but the work remains in a monastery museum near Sofia and speaks for the man who made it at the cost of his eyes, his very eyes. For history, epitaph enough, monument enough.

oses wrote that Adam wanted to know the nature of good and evil. Goethe wrote that Faust wanted to know all there was to know. Because Adam wanted to know more than he had a right to know, he lost Eden. Because Faust wanted to know no less than everything, he lost his soul. In both cases the obsessions or compulsions were not what could be called foreign to the experience of most men. At least I confess to them. The desire to know the nature of good and evil — not merely what is apparently good or what is apparently evil — is my preoccupation as much as it was Adam's. Frequently I would like nothing better than to know in advance of a decision or an action what the good or bad consequences will be or whether what I am deciding or doing is good or bad in itself. And I have lost Eden after Eden of my own peace of mind pursuing the delicious vanity of inscrutability. Moreover, the student that is still alive within me continues to want to know whatever is knowable. At times when my eyes burn from perusing page after page or when my mind aches and rocks with contradictions, I find myself thinking like Faust that omniscience would be infinitely preferable to the pursuit of truth in the endless process that is learning. So far I have not gambled my soul on it because I remain, as a matter of ground-level logic, irrefutably convinced of the fact that what I know will always be in arrears of what I do not know, which is probably the only absolute knowledge I have. Yet I am as vulnerable to arrogance and hauteur as any man. I have frequently confused righteousness with simply being in the right or mistaken a piece of the truth for all of it. At such times, like Adam and Faust, I've been out of touch with my soul, and by my standards that really amounts to losing it.

It should not be assumed that every attempt to exceed the limits of the possible is pre-ordained to end in failure. The impulse of Icarus and the fate of that effort are not by their very nature a part of an ongoing script of doom. In point of Icarian fact they are two separate considerations and should be considered separately. Granted, Icarus soared higher than he should have. Granted, his flight ended because of that miscalculation. But he certainly did not fly higher with the knowledge that he would fall. Had he known, really known, what would happen, he would have proceeded at a lower altitude and reached Sicily with his father. In which case we would have lost one of the most beguiling myths of the western world. No flight, no fall. No fall, no myth. No myth, no Icarus. Regardless, I choose to see the Icarian impulse as an act of faith. For Icarus it may have been no more than an act of faith in his wings. He acted on that faith. That he fell does not and did not denigrate that faith. Suppose he had succeeded as Lindbergh succeeded in an epic event that is internationally known or as Robert Beaman succeeded in a lesser known event, namely, the Olympic broad jump of 1968. Here was an athlete who had barely qualified for the finals. Having qualified, he found himself engaged in a sport where records are advanced, if they are advanced at all, by halves of inches or centimeters. But Beaman, with nothing but an athlete's faith in his trained body, made one leap and shattered by more than a foot the standing world record. Beaman himself, still caught up in that body-faith, reacted to the news of his achievement in total disbelief — a disbelief so genuine that it reduced him to tears, almost to blubbering. The desire was one thing; he could cope with that. The result was another; he had trouble coping with that. My concern is with the desire.

*R*ationality as a principle means nothing more than our capability to reason. It is certainly a capacity that distinguishes us from beavers, but it is not the only one. We can imagine, we can laugh, we can murder, we can waste time, we can decide to build a house totally different from the houses of our neighbors — all of which are beyond even the most precocious beaver. Thus to concentrate too mightily upon reason as all that "distinguishes us from the beasts" is not only to miss certain other distinctions but to make all our actions answerable to reason. This leads to rationalism, which is as much a debilitation of the mind as are sarcasm, cynicism and snobbery. Rationalism assumes that every human act, regardless of its nature, must in some way be thought of, thought through and subsequently thought about. It means more than this, to be sure, but it certainly means this much. One manifestation of it occurs, for example, in our experience of pain and pleasure. Why are we impelled to intellectualize or rationalize or otherwise attempt to "think" our pleasures while we do not do the same with pain? All we usually do with pain is accept it or endure it in the hope that it will end or be alleviated. But pleasures we do not accept fully until we give ourselves some reason why we should. It's as if we must find some rational justification for pleasures before we think we have the right to give ourselves to them. And even when we do find whatever it is that permits us to enjoy ourselves, our thinking, far from stopping, actually intensifies so that it tends to dull or dilute our enjoyment even during our experience of it. What does all this have to do with Icarus? It simply confirms in my mind that Icarus was not a rationalist. I see him more as an existentialist or even a romantic. I suspect that thinking too much — thinking things to death —

really bored him. That propensity may have suited his father, but Icarus was not so much a man of calculation as a man of the frontier. He had a boy's will, and he was vulnerable to those mistakes that result from enthusiasm. But he knew a challenge when he saw one. That he did not think through the consequences of his response to one challenge was his failing, his memorial and his right.

*O*ne of the principles of aerodynamics is that airplanes are kept aloft not by the uplift of air from beneath their wings but by the uptug of air across the tops of their wings. The physics of this principle mystifies me, but I accept it as I tend to accept most aerodynamic and other matters which I don't understand but which work, regardless. It also explains Pegasus to me. For years I've wondered why the Greeks chose a winged horse as a symbol for poetry. Because a horse is the most beautiful of animals, the most gracefully powerful? Or because the rhythm of the hooves of a horse in canter or gallop seemed to the Greeks linked to the rhythm of poems? My suspicion is that the Greeks understood that rhythm as such has the same lulling effect on human beings as routine has. Like routine, rhythm dulls as it lulls us so that it finally usurps our attention by linking us to its lockstep. When words are made to fit a predetermined rhythm, we eventually don't listen to what each word means or what a chain of words is saying. Those who write in this fashion create nothing but verse — groundlevel verse. It does not do what true poetry by its very nature can do. It does not rise. Enter Pegasus, the horse who flies. The rhythm of the hooves is there, but it is felt rather than heard when Pegasus crosses the sky. Suspended by the uptug of inspiration, Pegasus canters or gallops or cavorts on silent hooves as his mood takes him. His country is the universal air. Earthbound versifiers have no way of overtaking him or of rising to his level. He rides in his flight as long as his elevating inspiration sustains him, and he dominates us with the loud silence of his ride as surely as the blood in our vessels impresses its rhythms on our moods and acts and words (or vice-versa) without our really knowing how.

Slowly, much more slowly now and always by hand with pen and midnight ink, like checks made out to God, my poems come when they come. Lyrics of rejection score my pages, version after version. Like maps of countries that survive no more, each version dies in its successor just as water dies in steam, steam in air, and air into the fire that is all. Memorizing ashes, I go forward in reverse before a fate I almost can remember from a future that's already happened. My clockhands lock like exclamation points on midnight's noon. While I clock on to question marks, they lap me in the way fresh runners lap a tired runner on an oval. Subtracted from myself, I see my birthdays cancel out like algebra until I'm almost down to none. Then less than that, then none. Clocked free of facts, I learn that history is just the "victors' propaganda" while tomorrow's only gift is death. To pass the night I mimic in my way a moth with eyelash-legs and wings like tissue-ices melting back to air. Unwinged except with what my breath remembers of the wind, I live to search for God at dawn where else but in the heartbeat of the sun . . . Quartered now with polished surfaces and circuits that can pipe the news from France, ignite a bulb against oblivion or match the Fahrenheit of Spain in perpetuity, I crown myself the king of switches I refuse to switch. Like fire in a field, I burn in place to keep the night at bay. I touch the veins of rhododendrons breathing in the dark like wings of butterflies at rest. My palms remember breasts and doorknobs that remember them. I picture lovers, even as they fit and struggle and divide, as skeletons embracing skeletons. I summon from another snow the quiet scripture of my mother's smile. Grinding my thoughts to bone, I'm skinned to skullteeth clamping a cigar that smolders at its core the more it smolders down and dies into tomorrow like a star.

*P*aris declines behind the Loire. Next vanish Belgium, Switzerland and Luxembourg, becoming like the dense Ardennes just so much green and shadow on the shell of Babel. Spiking the clouds, the Alps say yesterday's a dream, tomorrow the dream of a dream, and I a dreamer in passage, dreaming. The lessons of the blood? Suspended. Below this plane where I am one passenger among two hundred, the globe slurs by, but where's the cast? History dissolves into geography the way real faith degenerates into religion. I have no difficulty seeing how bombardiers, like assassins armed with silencers, can kill from space. Through buffering blue, no screams, no glimpse of what their bombs bequeath to sirens and the spades and picks of crews, no rubble smoking like a swamp. The farther, the smaller; the smaller, the stranger; the stranger, the less significant: the less significant, the more ignorable; the more ignorable, the easier to see that seeing's not believing. Or is it more significant and less ignorable? Regardless, it's still what the believer sees. The night I saw the earth beamed by television from the moon, I learned anew what I knew I knew. Europe's jigsaw, ices on the poles, the slimming pork chop known as South America? Mt. Everest? Impressive as a pebble of the Parthenon. Later, my slow descending to Caracas by funicular remade the moon's point. Seaward, freighters at anchor in the harbor bobbed like navies in a bathtub. Beyond the Andes, Caracas bloomed as just so many roofs. No sheets on pulleys snapping in the sun, no Indians in burlap hawking orchids for a peso, no life but what I saw and named while being cable-carried roofward from a cable cast in Stuttgart. Which proved again what I'm re-proving now — that overviews are not perspective. Dangled from the cords of God and Pan American, I watch the still-life seven miles down bewitch me like a true believer's dream of heaven. When does it stop? When did it start? Why can't I see mirages? Earthward or upward, what's nearer than now or sooner than air? As for the far? It's always someone else's here. I'll see it when I get there.

What prompted me to keep on hiking through Rocquebrune and up the steepening paths and slopes to the cemetery is still not clear to me. After all, what was there to see but a grave? Was I merely being intrigued again by the propensity of certain great men of our time to be buried in remote villages — Churchill in Bladen, DeGaulle in Colombey-les-deux-Eglises, Jacques Maritain in Kolbsheim. Or was it because the cemetery itself was situated challengingly on the highest point of the mountain, higher even than the fourteenth century Carolingian castle that was supposed to dominate everything? Through the village I hiked, through the cramped streets walled in by the medieval closeness of the houses — a closeness that the architect whose grave I was hunting would probably have approved on military rather than architecturally innovative grounds. Beyond the village began the laps of sloping paths flanked by grapevines and waterfalls of bougainvillea. Far, far below the red tile rooves of the mountain houses glistened the bay of Rocquebrune where the architect himself had drowned after having suffered, according to reports, a heart attack while he was swimming. How just, I thought, to die quite literally at sea level and even below sea level and then be hearsed to the heights and buried among all the French and Italian residents of the village that was his home. And yet how ironic for a man whose life was devoted to the creation of interesting if not always beautiful spaces to end in such a crowded and tiered jam of baroque statuary and flamboyant gravestones that displayed in the European manner photographic cameos of those entombed beneath the stones. And finally when I found his grave after much searching amid the more majestic carvings over the bones of dead financiers and petite bourgeoisie, how lovely a royal blue stone awaited me on which was written in longhand, not carved, in French that I translated in the hot Mediterranean noon as "Here lies Edward Jenneret, known to the world as Le Corbussier."

*orget mythology. Forget the Greekishness of all this layered expli-
cation. What else is Icarus but the rise and fall of everything? Begin
with waves and how they mount into brackish, sundering ridges that charge
the beaches of this world like Neptune's cavalry before they shatter, spill
and froth, and Icarus is there. Or with your hand below your heart, feel how
the lungs uplift the ribs and then let them down, and Icarus is there. The
javelin, thrown and soaring and descending, is the arc of Icarus. The smell
of Icarus was in the first rock of Sodom and in the final ash of Troy. Icarus
is in the sail that cups the riding wind and carries it from cape to cape until
it calms, leaving the once fulfilled and surging sail as limp and lifeless as a
conquered flag. Icarus charts the way of human growth that ends not with
unchanging stature but with the slow shift and drop of our skin and our
innards gutward, earthward, graveward. And Icarus is the smirking spy who
hovers over the decline of some loves as when a women, no longer sexually
or otherwise interesting to her husband, begins to insist on respect as a mat-
ter of minimum right and finally settles for the last rites of jealousy, jiltings
and jewelry. And Icarus rules the temperate zones from April through No-
vember. Tulip spears, crocus question marks, the fresh gold of the forsythia
and the pastel rainbows of all the azaleas reach by fractions for the Icarian
sun. The leaves of apples, oaks and poplars gather and enlarge on branches,
hiding the skeletal wood with just enough of themselves to build a million
cages of leaf space before they finally fall, which really means a falling from
green to brown to orange to yellow from branch to ground, from mountain
to valley as the wind works its brooming will, leaving behind a pattern of
what ends so that something else can begin so that something else can end

so something else can begin. And there in the first and last green, in the seed
that dies so it can live, is Icarus.

atterhorn? Cervin? In fact, in photographs or in the woodcuts from Yvoire, it thrusts its granite tusk at Scorpio. The Jungfrau and Mont Blanc reach thinner air, but neither rears the same defiance at the stars. Dreaming that summit down, I christen it the alp of no retreat. Like some great tuning fork, it tongues real voices from the wind. "No pasarán," screams La Pasionaria. McSweeney shuns the jailer's cup and damns the British bread so he can perish Irish and free. Napoleon confronts his regiments and dares them, dares them to shoot, dares them to shoot their emperor. Shouting with rocks in either hand, a boy advances on advancing tanks in Belfast or Jerusalem . . . If I were higher than myself by half a Matterhorn, I'd see what these defiers saw. My quick predictable kilometers would shrink to roads adjoining roads adjoining roads. My old horizons would expand by hemispheres, by centuries. No by no, I'd find myself by losing what I never could become. Before sea-level reasons tugged me down, I'd swear by all the leaves in Switzerland that I would dare the sheerest mountain for the merest cause with nothing present but the air and nothing absent but applause.

Had the wax not melted on the wings of Icarus, I suppose he would have flown higher. How high? Who knows? Certainly, or almost certainly, as high as possible. Perhaps he might have sought the top of the sky until he realized that there was no top or until his failure to realize it forced him into a downing crash with some other law of physics. What would have lured him to climb? Desire, probably. He might have just wanted to do it. Which immediately suggests to me that wanting and wanting more mean the same thing. What is wanting if not a quest for satiety, and what is satiety but the glut of surfeits? It is never moderate. Always there is the itch for more skill, more recognition, more power, more pistachios, more love, more money. More money! Let capitalism be our metaphor then. Here is a system whose frank and laudably realistic purpose is to legitimize the daily voracity of human greed. What makes a capitalist? Capital, obviously. No matter how much capital a capitalist has, he wants or at least would not refuse more. And he seeks more by aggrandizing or conserving what he already has. He has an embellisher's eye and an embellisher's cunning. Profitable speculation and saving are his motives. If profitable speculation means gambling, saving means not merely hoarding. It also means looking for bargains, which means retaining capital that would otherwise be spent, which gives the saver the capitalistic satisfaction that he is beating a system whose first law is to make cheap and sell dear. Regardless, there is no top to the amasser's sky, and every capitalist is an amasser. The answer to a little more is a lot more and, afterward, still more. And why shouldn't Icarus find a place there? Everything that is more than enough summons him.

From this amoeba's ocean, black and bottled, I prepare to fish my life. I pantomime Picasso poised above his paints. Or Dr. Schweitzer just before I thumb the hypodermic plunger down and suck the pen-blood home. Primed, I wait for anything to happen — doodles, numbers, circles, parallelograms. The pen won't paint or play until it scrawls its way to what I'm writing now. I feel like Icarus in full flight, abandoned to the medium of wings, more like something flown than someone flying. The lines I write create each other like a script without a plot. I tell my hand to tell the pen to stop. Capped and clipped to my shirt pocket, the pen keeps writing in my mind. The blood won't clot. Almost out loud I ask what's in the script. The pen keeps busy writing. Is there a script or not? The pen writes on. It suddenly occurs to me that I'm the script. And if I am, who's writing me? And why? And where? And for how long?

*M*y shirts and trousers? Hang them like a dead man's wardrobe in a closet marked anonymous. My keys? Melt them to rods with which the mad can beat the sea. My books and papers? Box them like ancient atlases of how my world looked once. My house? In half a thousand Aprils, only the ants will mortgage it. My wish? To see how much I can deny before I'm left with nothing more than me between myself and nothing — to strip to the wits the way a man strips naked on a beach and prances out to sea or flaps his feathered arms for a sky-swim. Free.

What used to be a statue rubbles a patio around its pedestal. Like autumn chestnuts picked by gravity, these breakings lie as left, as found. They challenge me to re-imagine them as Dante frowning at the Florentines, as Venus with her hands concealing tandem privacies above her waist and one below, as some conquistador determined to be known in stone as anything that dared or dares destruction just because it happened. Sculpting through my dreams, I am of possibilities the very prince, a Michelangelo with God's okay to prove that nothing but everything comes from nothing, an Icarus whose past becomes a future that is always happening. All this — provoked by smithereens. What isn't there comes true as differently and clearly as my memories of students by the hundreds grown, graduations ago, into their promises. They re-create themselves behind my eyes before my eyes. They halt me name by name and face by face as suddenly as lightning interrupts and brightens to a halt the sky, demanding that the world stand still, that clocks stand still, that everything stand still until this very minute becomes all minutes past and ever. The lightning stops to leave me all at once in Paris on any night before tomorrow. DeGaulle himself drives by me in an open Peugeot on the Boulevard Raspail. Like some lost statue sculpted from the air, he meets my stare again because I see him there — because I saw him there.

Buckminster's bubble? Burned. Bowling a flowering inferno in its core, it sizzled skeletal and melted like the Hindenburg. Charred escalators twisted into stairs from hell. The silver latticework of crisscrossed steel became a black unsurface for the rain, the wind, the leaves. Nicole announced that Bucky's planet might become a planetarium. In seven years, fresh ivy could conceal the scorch. In ten, wisteria could pile and interweave and bloom from pole to pole. In twenty, who from Montreal's world's fair could prophesy how a newer world would fare? The earth's largest hothouse? A new terrarium with rainbows of exotica within its global walls? Nicole and I punned on in her "anglais" and my "franglais," creating from the ashes of an old man's biospheric dream a dream of phoenixes that kept ascending and ascending.

omething of the blind, impetuous courage of Icarus reminds me of those who fight the battle for the future now and lose, of those who risk seeming the fool for justice, of those who have bravery of heart, of those who knowingly take the path of most resistance, not because the difficult is always synonymous with the good, but because it is the only path for them in their circumstances to take, of those who have the courage of lost causes. What is important to them is the act, not the consequences. They can often be faulted for their prudence but not for their valor. They are not among the survivors of this world because the Falstaffian code of discretion and equivocation strikes them as an excuse for postponement or a ruse of cowardice. They are rather of the blood of heroes and tragedians of an epic cut. So, a silent toast, please, for those who, simply by resisting, made the Alamo the Alamo, for those four hundred Spartans who stalled with their lives the surge of thousands of Persians at a niche named Thermopylae so that the Greek navy could later finish the job, for those forgotten Frenchmen who would not surrender in the cold Vercors, for Antigone and Juliet and Desdemona and not Ophelia and Ismene, for Clarence Darrow at his worst or best, for Lincoln just for being Lincoln, for what the Royal Air Force accomplished on that summer Sunday of the blitz when they fought without reserves and stopped the bombing of Britain by day, for Martin Luther King, Jr., on the march with garbage men in Tennessee, for all whose life in prospect seemed surrounded by impossibilities but in retrospect suddenly becomes a solution.

To die by natural causes describes and so suits the death of leaves as they surrender in their annual shrivel with such a gradual turn of color. It is never a quick shift from green to earth-tan. Nor does it start from green. All summer short even the green keeps changing from the first mantis-green of infant leaves to the billiard-table-top-green of the adult leaf. It is this green that is the currency of trees from late June through August and beyond. Then the green deepens into forest green, a green that painters create by mixing blue and yellow and a drop or two of black, the green of pre-death. Then the first crimson inks the jagged perimeters of oak leaves or the starfish leaves of silver maples. Soon afterward comes the tinct of copper and ochre and a beige that is more than beige. The leaves fold in upon themselves like hands gripping coins in their palms. The beige gives way to gold, and the gold in weeks molts to brown. Only the Japanese maple resists the common rainbow of decay, keeping its summer maroon until the first chill of September or October prods the maroon to wine and then the wine illogically to green, to tan, to brown tissue bits. In the end the wind has its way with everything on the branches of every tree except the conical firs, while the fallen and blown harvest of oak, elm, maple, ash, cherry, apple, sumac, sycamore and birch toss in an autumn salad of sere and whirled glory.

rom where I wait the climb of dawn, the first sun happens like the echo in the sky of a great fire in the Appalachians. My wedge of Pennsylvania keeps clocking toward it minute by second until it reaches the exact instant when the upper orange rim tips above the furze of the eastern horizon. The hot yellow fan of light surges out into the waiting sky like ink seeping solely upward into a blue blotter. And still the earth swirls slowly until the sun becomes its complete self. I know that the rise — but it is not an actual rise — will hallucinatingly go on to the apogee of noon, creating for everything and everyone beneath it a world spared for one second only of shadows. Then the illusion of descent will start because of the counter-clocking of the satelliting earth. The shadows will become longer than the objects that create and project them, and the west will wait for the last light as quietly as a grandfather too old to give a damn about death will wait for death. So much for evening and its fears. Now in the early sunsweep I'm suddenly reminded of a dawn when I was a passenger on a DC-9 en route from Pittsburgh to New York. The visibility at take-off on that stormy morning was less than a mile, and the rain splashed, streaked and speckled the portholes on the fuselage, which seemed more and more like oar-ports, as we took to the air. I watched the washed wings quiver while we surged higher, and I kept imagining how the jet, as it pushed loudly toward its cruising altitude through reefs of close, dirty clouds, reminded me of a sub-marine surfacing quickly in an emergency. All at once we broke through and over layered reefs, and there, all around and above us was the clean, dry sky where it had been all the time, and the morning was blazing up and over us like music. That night, when I returned on the same plane, I felt the darkness closing in and down on the plane like a cap on a cup. Far below, it was still evening, and I could see a slithering of the last, almost horizontal seeping of sunshine. But at our altitude there was only the dark, which kept descending with us from midnight at the sky's crown to the matching indigo that was catching up to midnight on the ground.

The burning house is tinder, nothing but tinder, and the fire huddled in its fierce and orange hive the way a tulip's core hides in the hub of the tulip's petals. The roof capsizes rather than collapses, and the roof fire bursts even higher all at once. Wall by caving wall, what used to be a house — a space where lives happened every day and every night — becomes the fuel of its own destruction. From every fresh collapse the fire sucks an impetus it never knew it had and climbs, climbs, climbs until it breaks into a whirl and spray and dally of sparks at the false height of its tallest flames. A year or more of building plus decades of dwelling, eating, sleeping, loving, sweating, suffering and just being becomes the kindling and memory of an hour. By some lithe magic of the mind, I re-focus so that I am watching not an incinerating house but the rise and fall of empires, Roman or otherwise, the firebombing of Hamburg, which begot Coventry, which begot Dresden, the passing of the carefully conceived and the painstakingly built into an instant's conflagration. Thus epochs. Thus the life of Icarus. Thus anything that mimes the slow upbuilding and the faster than imagined collapse. Thus even the sudden chickenkill when the hen, beheaded cleanly by the hatcheteer, does not realize it is already dead. Headless, it veers and careens about with much flapping of wings and spraying of neckblood. Soon its death catches up with it, and it turns dead for good so that in a matter of minutes there is enacted the crazy, soloing firedance of its dying and, finally, a death so absolute that the white layered feathers in the bloodied wings twitch in the wind like campfire ashes startled by a breath.

If Icarus means anything, he means that we desire experience, or rather we desire the experience of experience unencumbered by prudence, which implies that we desire the heretofore unexperienced. This comes down to the hankering in us to proceed from what we know to what we don't know since the desire for experience is usually the desire for the not yet known or at least the desire for the known reknown freshly. To let the body go on where only the imagination has had the courage to venture, that is the lure. To let the mind catch up later, as it invariably does, sorting, justifying, rejecting, remembering, that is the consequence. Experience is thus not knowledge. It is simply experience. It is what occupies us totally at the moment. Its fruit is awareness. Granted, experience that is never thought about is never completely or partially understood. Thus experience in this sense has us rather than vice-versa. Granted, the romantic is he who hungers for experience without grasping what experience teaches so that life for the romantic is nothing but a sequence of episodes in subsequence. Granted as well that experience does not fill us with understanding simply because it happened to us. We must think about it. And it is this thinking that creates a knowledge that derives from perspective, and it is this knowledge that is the prelude to understanding and the dry, tough eucharist of wisdom. But this comes later. And the Icarus in us is not concerned with the later. He is too busy obeying the body's imperative, which wants the fullest awareness and satisfaction right now. The mind's primary impulse is to adjudicate this awareness and measure this satisfaction, to make sense even where there may not be sense. And we are poised between the two and are compelled to live with the tension. We yearn for experience without responsibility, but the need to come to terms with it is ineluctable. What is usually sacrificed in the effort to come to terms is the spontaneity of the experience as and when it happened. It is reminiscent of the spontaneity that is destroyed when the intimate is made public. It loses in mystery what it gains in notice as is the case with whispers, nudism or sexual intercourse. But the mind is oblivious. Mystery is its enemy because mystery leaves it in suspense. Vexed, it is unable to judge and unwilling to acknowledge that the mystery of life even in the face of sheer absurdity is often what life really is. No matter. Icarus is there to remind us that the yet to be experienced moment waits only for the experiencer regardless of consequences. That is the invitation. He asks us to enter the moment.

The beauty of beauties to the Mayans was a cross-eyed girl, which proves that beauty was as much in the eye (or the eyes) of the beheld as the beholder. More literal in our century, we labor to correct such deviations from the not altogether okay because — . Because? Because we must, we feel we must. And why? So that all examples of the nakedly unusual can look as much like us as possible. If the values and standards of the Mayans appear to stand in contradiction to such a compulsion, why should we worry about the indictment of a civilization safely dead? After all, weren't these a people whose top award to victorious athletes was decapitation? We, the victory-addicted, ignore the fact that there might have been some hidden symbolism in this. Perhaps the Mayans wanted to cut off, as it were, victory's inebriating hubris in the bud as a reminder to man that he finds his true measure not in triumph but defeat. But such an amalgam of winning losers and headless victors leaves us as perplexed as the notion that crossed eyes could ever have been regarded as a beauty mark. Better, we say, to consign such to the hermetic harmlessness of the definite past in the same spirit in which we think of Egyptian antiquity, blinking the fact that sphinx-like sculptures of man as having the body of a lion topped by a human head may not have been far from the predatory truth about us. But the Mayans will somehow not go away. Their seemingly pointless stairways to the sun intrigue us. And their belief that their ancestors were winged men who founded cities in the Yucatan leaves us wondering. The crouched, bird-like warriors that they carved and colored on the friezes of their temples were Icaruses of sorts, descendant in the Mayan vision rather than ascendant in the Greek, but they are creatures of the air, as we all are, nonetheless.

Icarus rules the kingdom called Almost. Its citizens are determined but defeated has-beens and all others who learn to live, as well as they can manage, with their losses. If this seems to describe all the living, so be it. If it touches on a theme that sounds familiar, so be it as well since, finally, no other theme exists. Among the kinsmen and kinswomen of Icarus are, of course, the military dead of both victorious and vanquished armies, the blind, the dead, the halt, the risk-takers for even the most menial of motives, the few who live forbearingly with pain of either the body or the soul, the lonely who know the long thoughts that only solitude can create, the poets who believe that a poem without inspiration is like lovemaking without passion, the students who may be as honestly wrong as most car-clocks but who recover from it, thinkers who are able to resist the good intentions within their own malices, parents who find it difficult to let go and parents who do not and for those other parents I've never met who know the difference, women whom no one loved enough to marry and who wait like books in a library for someone to read them and so put them in circulation and bring them to life, the unlucky in cards, the never fully appreciated. Each of these Icarians is as near to each of us as air, even nearer. Look into any mirror anywhere at any time and this Icarus will stare back at you.

hy do they do it? I refer to the jugglers, wire-walkers, sleight-of-handers and daredevils of this world. Indentured to a daring of their own devising, they strive to match wits or skills with what is uselessly possible — the trick of keeping six spinning plates in the air simultaneously, a stroll on a cable stretched between the monoliths of the now destroyed World Trade Center, a fling of dagger after dagger at a woman in sequins spread-eagled on a turning circumference, a quick arc of someone fired from a cannon into a waiting net. Perhaps these riskers have no other motive than to prove again and again their own dexterity or nerve in a circumstance of melodramatic or contrived danger. Perhaps this may have something to do with their wanting to relish the ersatz fame known as notoriety. Perhaps they merely wish to create or re-create themselves anew with each performance in a way that is both untransferable and never exactly repeatable. Regardless, all such acts, like the acts of learning or loving, have the reward of being their own reward. Beyond braggadocio or hoopla or pizazz, we look at these doings, at least briefly, with some of the same amazement that is begotten in us by such other uselessly possible achievements as sculptures, paintings, designs, dramas or poems. But back to the riskers . . . Why do they do what they do? Is the motive hidden somewhere in that sometimes quixotic but ultimately universal need in man for the indispensable futility of the presently necessary? Necessary for what? For survival? No. For what then? For the doing, naturally.

*L*ife or longevity? We can't have both, but we live often in the belief that they are synonymous and not contradictory. Life, whatever else it may be, means ripeness in the present moment, and such ripeness is not prolongable as long as ripeness means ripeness. Longevity, of course, merely means many years of being alive (call it survival), and this is finally as much a matter of luck as it is of genes. Yet the urge to survive rather than live ripely is not to be taken lightly. Let statues be our metaphor for a moment. Statues are made with the intentions of enduring as if the sculptor is determined to let stone or bronze or steel do what is clearly impossible for flesh, blood, and bones. The intention here (as well as the illusion) is to show that what lasts must of necessity have real worth. I differ. As much as I admire the calm-eyed seated kings of Luxor and Karnak, I admire even more and for totally different reasons the ice sculptures of Sapporo and Montreal. In short, my criterion is that beauty and perpetuity are not as memorable as beauty and eternity, and I hasten to add that eternity to me does not represent a long time but is whatever and wherever time is not. In this spirit I marvel at ice sculptures of Europa and the bull or ice statuettes of the Eiffel Tower not only because they testify to the artist's skill in such a cold medium but because the maximum effort, as with weddings, is made with no temporal expectations and minimum temporal return. After all, the ice will melt, and the handiwork will cease to exist except in the memories of those who saw and appreciated frozen water cut in such shapes. Posterity be damned. Some things are made for the making, and that, in art or in life, is or should be enough. But it isn't.

*C*all him, for the purpose of this story, Ben. Having immigrated as a boy with his slightly older brother to the United States from Lebanon, he grew up not really as an American but as a Lebanese in America. It made no difference that he eventually became a citizen of the United States and that he worked at a county job until he qualified for a pension. His orientation remained foreign. And the real reason for this was that he wanted to return to his mountain village in the Levant in his twilight years as an immigrant who had "made it." The pension would permit him to live without working, and he imagined himself basking in the envy of the other villagers. And in due time he, after burying his brother, took his pension and returned to what he always called the "old country." For Ben this was the climax of his life, a triumphant return, a rise from nothing to something. But once in the village of his birth, he found that the villagers not only did not envy him but held him in silent contempt because he tried to lord his importance over them and seemed to expect something like obeisance or deference from them. In a matter of months he became isolated, and within a year he suffered a stroke that not only left him unable to take care of himself but ultimately drained him of his monthly pension so that only the kindness and charity of the villagers kept him alive. Neighbors would see to it that he was fed and washed and not left alone. One can only imagine how a stroke-muted man must have responded to this undeserved concern from people whom he expected at one time to treat him like a king. If he were of a mind to thank them, he could not. If he were of a mind to refuse or scorn them, he could not. When he died, the villagers had to take up a collection to pay for his funeral. And that closed it — a life whose fall was in its rise. The rest was predictable.

If poetry is what T. S. Eliot presumed it to be — "the best words in the best arrangement" — then it really is no more than the best conversation of which we are capable. Such heightened conversation certainly should not always be associated with the printed page, the formal reading or the honorific occasion. Where else then? Why not those times in our lives when rising to the occasion is called for: the toast, the curse, the compliment, the condolence, the riposte? The toast, for example, presumes the toastmaster will memorialize the passing moment by being its tongue. When the moment and the inspiration strike fire in the right person, the result is poetry, as in Churchill's deservedly famous tribute to the Royal Air Force ("Never in the field of human conflict has so much been owed by so many to so few.") or John F. Kennedy's equally famous welcome to the Nobel Prize winners in Washington ("I think this is the most extraordinary collection of talent or human knowledge, that has ever been gathered together in the White House, with the possible exception of when Thomas Jefferson dined alone.") or Nikos Kazantzakis' less well known but no less able huzzah to life ("Greetings, man, you little two-legged plucked cock! It's really true — don't listen to what others say — if you don't crow in the morning, the sun does not come up!"). Among many nationalities the curse is something of an art form. Far from being a bilious purgation, the rather limited range of most cussers in America is often as predictable, repetitive and unimaginative as pornography with or without the expletives deleted. (The deletions, at least, permit the reader some room for imagination). For contrast, I offer the following by Robert Desnos, which is to pedestrian swearing what Cyrano is to Montfleury: "Cursed be the father of the bride of the blacksmith who forged the iron for the axe with which the woodsman hacked down the oak from which the bed was carved in which was conceived the great-grandfather of the man who was driving the carriage in which your mother met your father!" As for compliments, most move quickly toward overstatement, or collapse into flattery. This was certainly not true of Jan Sibelius' remark to Marian Anderson after she gave a concert in his honor in his own home: "Miss Anderson, the roof of my house is too low for you." And what of the triteness of our condolences? Good eulogies are rare: most are as pathetic as Hallmark verse. Again, for contrast, consider Georges Pompidou's spare announcement of the death of Charles de Gaulle: "Tonight France is a widow." As for the riposte, we often lack the quickness that prompted one Parisian hostess who, when insulted by an uninvited guest's remark that "Her meal was fit for a pig," was able to respond evenly, "I'm so glad you felt at home." Nor should any of these utterances from toast to riposte be said with any touch of smuggery. Rather they should be thrown away like Jean-Claude Killy's answer after he was asked by a reporter if winning three gold medals at Grenoble qualified as the highest moment in his life. "In my sporting life," Killy answered calmly. This has the intentional self-deprecation that I associate with the vexing habit of the American poet William Stafford to choose with forethought the least flattering photographs of himself for the jackets of his books or the practice of oriental weavers who deliberately weave one imperfection into their rugs to acknowledge that perfection is only possible for God and leave it go at that.

*I*t makes no difference that I can't remember what I ought to write or that my life is less a saga than I like. Tonight I read the constellations with my son. He counts the Pleiades and comes up short by one, outlines Orion and his sword and then picks with a hunter's grin the blue ruby that is Venus. Under the nimbus of another moon, Magellan's constellations helped loop the world Columbus created. Radar can do it better and surer now, though radar blips, framed on the ticking sky of some navigator's screen, manage still to look curiously star-like. So, the difference between the astrolabe and electronics is really a difference in degree, not kind, at least to my way of dreaming. My son is adding Sirius and Betelgeuse and Sculptor to his catch and asking me how high the North Star is. I say there is no high or low in space, just near and far. He doesn't ask me to explain, and he seems satisfied a while. I hope we won't get into light years, which are time's way of telling space and which boggle me into a silence I try to avoid. Suddenly, looking up (or rather out into space), I find myself thinking of the whole speckled panorama as the total count of God's pins or as a zillion mounted lightning bugs pinched dead in the very act of lighting. It makes me want to take the paper money of inconsequence in my palm and shape it with my kneading fingers into a wad the size of a marble and shuck it permanently. Schooled by my son or schooling in return, I shrink beneath the sum of every torch that man and myth have named in one immensity — each star a marriage of far fact and the dubbing wands of many imaginations. Sirius, Betelgeuse, Sculptor, the Dippers, the twelve moons of Jupiter and the nine moons of Neptune all announce themselves within the kingdom of the night's white sun. We name them together like

Daedalus and Icarus brought up to date while dawn, that murderer of stars and melter of dreams, waits to offer once more for the first and last time the holy sacrifice of the world.

*A*float, they seem to be standing horizontally at attention, toes pointing at the clouds, shoulder blades pressed to the buoying mattress of water that beds them supine with their eyes aimed at nothing but Mediterranean blue. Like brooms they float. They seem to possess a ballast of kapok or cork. Soap-men, woodmen, feather-men, men unsinkable as Ping-Pong balls, men beyond the fear or even the possibility of submersion, they almost nap as the soft swells roll under them in a tilt that is only possible for great bodies of water in slow motion. Snoozing on Solon's sea, they would understand Solon's saying "The sea is stirred by the wind: if it be not stirred, it is the quietest of all things." These floaters seem part of the sea at one moment and at another just so much breathing flotsam. Ashore, at tables capped by rainbow parasols on steel poles, men and women from everywhere but Monaco are talking flags, talking pesos or francs, talking oils made especially for sunning, talking drinks they will have before dinner. Chaired on the earth, they are busy with chat, chat, chat and pauses before more chat. They bury themselves in chat, drown in chat, thrash in chat. Passing their tables, I can hear them sinking. But the small armada of tilting floaters in the shallows lets the world come to them as cleanly as the sky touches the sea. Beneath them the measured fathoms are nothing but upholders, nothing but what the floaters need right now to make their vision of the uppermost blue in the sunfan straight above them something they'll remember as a time when leisure's nectar never tasted sweeter. Backs in brine and foreheads to the wind, they are both over and under the circumstances. The water coasts them, and the sky never ends.

The shortsightedness of Prometheus! To steal fire from heaven and bring it to earth, thereby giving man the chance to create the only element he can create, was to give man god-like options. Unlike Icarus, who aspired to heaven and tried to wing his way there, Prometheus opted for the reverse. A refugee from heaven, he wanted to share something of that heaven with men. The gift was fire, but in all his fore-thinking could Prometheus have anticipated what the gift would bring, make possible, undo? Cooking, to be sure. No longer at the mercy of the raw and bloody, we were and are able to fork our way from grilled fish and heated vegetables to the primest of prime steaks. With campfires we can hold back darkness. We furnace ores and pour them cooling into molds that yield us chalices, knives, rings and crowns. We blow the taffy goo of hot glass into the best of flagons. We bake with electric suns the skin of our very bodies, bring summer into zero rooms and sizzle with a plunged torch the rattler in his nest. We light our way with candles through the mistiest of attics, and with the trayed twins of the same candles we create the atmosphere of sacraments. But from the same heat and with the same light we hue the shaped steel of tools and weapons. Thus, peace. Thus, war. There is no doubt that we could still remain peaceful without the hammer, chisel, nail and file. But without the bullet, bomb and bayonet the fact of war as we know it would vanish like a bad dream. By reverse logic it is possible to conclude that all wars from the days of the sword to the age of the missile are the creation of steel, which is the creation of fire, which is the gift of Prometheus, which is why the fore-seeing gods probably chose to punish him for sharing the divine element with creatures who would find some way to pervert it.

Whatever I imagine turns to zero. Whatever I remember I forget like outdoor laundry left to midnight and the moon. I'm tired of towns where everybody dresses differently but thinks and dreams alike. I'm sick of news the information mills crank out and on and on like porno theaters that never close. I've had enough of all who live by compromise, and that means everyone but children and the mad. I'd like the best to happen by itself — like poetry. But even poetry's not listening. What's left? What's right if I'm so stuck that nothing stirs me — not Berlioz, not telegrams at dawn, not lightning, not the cheekflesh of a breast against my side. To match my mood I think of beached canoes or flags so slack that they're not flags at all or quicksand sucking at my knees like mouths. The more I sink the more I struggle. Struggle, and the more I sink. With breathing as my last choice to wage against the odds, I see in this dark death of sorts a preface to a life that lasts. If it's the death of rocks, I'm destined for the cold eternity of diamonds. If it's the death of seeds, the air will be my future and my present and my past.

*F*or one psychologist the plunge of Icarus was symbolic of the sub-merging of the psyche. In a word, depression — the squelching of desire — the antithesis of ecstasy. Let ecstasy then be the ascending, harmonious fulfillment of desire. Not euphoria. Not the mindless gloat of seeming well-being. I mean true ecstasy as when the mind suddenly realizes its own power and focuses itself as a mind — as when lovers approach and then reach that release when their bodies seem to be feeding and feeding on one another in motions that are beyond mere willing but are nonetheless what the will wants and wanted from the beginning. Imagine then the op-posite — the clamping down on all possible epiphanies — the keyless jails of denial for the sake of denial — the slammed door of suppression. Imagine then the difference between man in air and man in water, and you sense for a moment the difference between soaring and squelching. That is why Icarus becomes the first and only promise of our kind, psychology notwith-standing. We either rise or not. Everything else is drowning.

Instead of boulevards I see the roofs of drowned buses. Telephone poles resemble masts of schooners scuttled in a row or Christian crosses rising from the river's morgue. Uptown, I tally floating fifths of river beer, two cats riding a plant downcurrent, sodden mattresses, tires clogged with silt, a dead hen slimed slick — and traffic bulbs still blinking red, amber and green at taxies flooded to the plugs. Ebbing, the river leaves its jetsam on the curbs like gulped junk gutted from the bellies of a thousand sharks. Curb by curb, the surface of the street re-surfaces. Around a sweatered, bloated pekinese, powwowing pigeons strut and bow like oriental generals. Following the shrinking riverline, the sun mops up ahead of one blind believer on the march. Testing the river's cellar with her staff, she wades through clutter and impossibilities. Why is she here? Where is she heading? Invisible, I watch her as I'd watch some pilgrim hiking miles to a miracle. Her dead eyes dream of no horizons. Her cane-wand, thimbled with rubber, lightens her way by touches. Tap by tap, she teaches me that innocence alone can walk these dryways and survive. If I were blind enough to see, I might agree. But I've been taken by surprise too often to be off my guard. I look. I watch my step. Convinced that tides will drown us after all, I settle like a docked and anchored scow. The girl with the cane sails by, sails on, sails free across Gennesaret. Sighting on blind faith, she tacks or trims to the wind's shim and the tricks of her possible sea.

t is invariably forgotten that Eiffel himself, Eiffel of the tower, designed the infrastructure of steel and iron for the statue. The statue itself, paid for and donated to the Americans by the people of Paris, measures one hundred and fifty-one feet. Statue and pedestal together — the pedestal being the contribution of the Americans — rise to a height of three hundred and five feet. Even by the standards of 1886, the entire undertaking was formidable and confirmed again the French genius for the symbolically exact. Bartholdi, the commissioned artist, stipulated that Eiffel's iron skeleton be covered by three hundred copper plates and that each plate should be exactly 3/32 of an inch thick. Once completed and erected, the structure was called the Statue of Liberty, and it both duplicated and dwarfed its sister sculpture near the Tuilleries in Paris. The head of the statue, crowned by an illuminated spiked nimbus, remains generically classical, specifically Roman. With a torch in the upraised right hand, a cracked shackle at her feet and a tablet with a date in the left hand, the Statue of Liberty was the first sight that shipborne incomers had of the United States of America. A record of the expressions on the faces of these immigrants exists in photographs taken of them from 1900 to 1910. Usually the photographs show men, women and children crowded at the rail of a ship. They are not aware that they are being photographed. The sight of the Statue of Liberty does something to their eyes — heightens, softens and somehow brightens them into the eyes of children on the eve of a feast or of believers, believing.

*O*nce born, once named, the myth of Icarus faded into the future that is now our history. Fading, it became itself again in a series of different resurrections, and each resurrection faded in turn into its successors as fathers fade into their sons and as these sons, when fathers, fade into their sons. So faded Thebes and Delphi into ruins, into archeology, into whatever we now know of them or will know. Similarly fade the smoke of campfires and explosions, the smoke named recollection or the bitter smoke of fear, the smoke of breath at zero or the misting haze of exhalations against glass. Turn one full circle and confront all the fading houses on the farthest hill we can manage to see, see clouds fading in full scud, hear cars that pass and leave the fast echo of where they just were, follow the fadeaway of high sky into low sky, the ocean from shallow green to deeper emerald to topaz to charcoal, remember the backyard shout that fades before we hear it like a hammersmack in another county, the 707 that is just beginning its approach, parting the unpatched sky like some unique air-fish, descending and fading into a horizon that is someone else's zenith or count the roads that are fading and wearing down and back to earth again. What is age but the fading out of years into years that become the past even as we reach them so that we think finally that life is nothing but one slow or fast fade into whatever death is. We try to remember what we can't help but forget — names, faces, birthdays, old addresses. We have to think twice before we can recall our own age. Writing suddenly becomes our way to put something down that solves the confusion for the moment. Someone may read it before the ink fades or the page turns into powder. No monuments then, no huzzahs, no tribute but the smoke of memory. Heraclitus was correct. Each one of us within his skin is burning. The temperature inside the wrists, the thighs, the loins or the chest is but one degree and a fraction under one hundred. And we burn. Since all fires need air to go on being fire, we follow the law of fire. In air we burn. Watching fires, we watch something of the shadow of ourselves — the slow start, the fierceness of the full inferno, the contending flames, the banking and the smoldering that shrinks into ash that keeps for so long the memory of its orange glory. This is the element that is always present, never past. The fire is as we are. The smoke of our legacies is already disappearing unless in some imagined vision we can transcribe them for the eyes, the ears, the very blood of those who will come and vanish after us. Shakespeare at fifty-two was dead with all those plays and all that poetry behind him. That much remains Shakespeare in perpetuity like a diamond that Vulcan himself cannot smelt.

Baptized as Giovanni, he became the saint we know as Francis. Why? Because his father thought Francesco would impress his customers in France much more than Giovanni. And it apparently did. It's not unusual. By error, choice or evolution, names survive along the way not always as given but as transformed. Aluminium, so the story goes, became aluminum because a printer inadvertently removed the "I." The "S" in Harry S. Truman stands for nothing. Tracing his roots to Tuscany, John Ciardi explained how Gerhardt altered to Gerardi to Ciardi. But what's the point? Unless a name reflects the essence of a thing, what good's a name? For example, who can find a better word for treachery than treachery, murder than murder, tango than tango, gossip than gossip? When foreigners or children improvise or err, the outcome's often better: "lapkin" for napkin, "wristlegs" for ankles, "teethbrush" for toothbrush. It seems that naming the world is our compulsion. And yet what else is poetry but searching for and finding a word that says what something really is and means?

he wind turned wild as a raving hag determined to be heeded and unwilling to be stilled. It made a sapling of an ancient oak before the oak just snapped. It twirled the trees still left with leaves until they swirled like flagellants insane with God. Just when it seemed to fade, it tripled in fury. Watching in all our impotence, we saw much more than the wind called the mistral. To some of us the trees were proof that force could be withstood just as pressure is withstood. Or pain. Others foresaw revenge from heaven on the loose. For reasons they could not explain still others thought of soldiers weathering bombardment on a beach. We all were wrong. Who needed a Mediterranean wind to tell us we discover who we are in anguish, that God and vengeance are at odds despite what we attribute to creation, that seeing what the wind evokes is best left to poetry? But still we kept on listening as if to an orchestra of flutes played by the insane. We had no choice. Like omens or threats, the wind commanded nothing less than our absolute attention. Poetry would have to wait.

The push of contradictions crush us, and we shatter. Not that it matters to the world at large. The airports stay busy. Quintuplets born in Winnipeg survive, and wars continue to happen because they continue to happen. The issue is that contradictions unexposed or unrefuted manage to prevail as facts that no one challenges. The central sun, for instance, stays still, which means it never sets or rises. Judges sentence the condemned without qualm to three consecutive life terms. In France the twin born last is called the older. People who know a lot and qualify as wise (although there's no connection) simply go along. To contradict what's contradictory hardly needs defending, but the price is steep. Consider Socrates whose only crime was asking why. Or James Augustine Joyce whose sin was forging from the smithy of his soul the permanent defiance of his books. Or General Smedley Butler who refused to send marines to battle for bananas in the Caribbean. What did they reap for being right but ridicule or worse? But when they were safely buried, suddenly the accolades were global, posthumous — and cheap.

Today I have nowhere to go and nothing to do but watch the Mediterranean sea from a seaside table in Menton. Nobody knows me here. The couples dancing tangos in the public square regard me as the foreigner I am. I order lunch in unimpressive French and sign language. The world that pressured me at home with phone calls, obligations, bills and headlines carries on, but I'm not playing. Instead I focus on the green and red confusion of a nicoise salad while I hurt for an America I barely recognize. In the name of Jesus Christ we're Arabizing Arabs as we tried to Vietnamize the Vietnamese forty years ago. We've sacrificed thousands for a policy based on vanity and guns. Elsewhere we sponsored free elections where Samson died and reversed results. To launch the neo-century we crushed a country and destroyed a culture. Though someone warned that occupiers lose at last, the warning was ignored. When scholars wrote that Athens at its peak sailed fleets to ultimate catastrophe in Sicily and bled for decades afterward into inconsequence, they reaped nothing but the glory of derision. Citing history with those whose only purpose is deceit is futile. Hiding behind lapel-pin flags, they've fouled what I hoped would be a holiday abroad, not merely a reprieve before the next resistance. It's nothing new. I've met their kind a thousand times whenever fear or cowardice demanded that I be loyal to causes that were never mine. Since power has always been their word for peace, they swagger like competitors who simply can't not win. But when they lose, as they will always lose, they'll claim they could have won with more support from those who disagreed, and then they'll whine.

My bags are packed and trunked, the gas tank brimmed, the route pre-chosen and the weather clear. I savor an Icarus moment that everyone tastes just before a trip. I've washed and waxed the car and tire-shined each tire to a gloss. Call it a quirk, but I prefer possessions or surroundings up to scratch: shoes buffered, trousers pressed so that the creases cut, shirts laundered to the purest white. A wall picture hung askew disturbs me. I bridle at misspellings in a published book. In brief, whatever's disproportionate or out of place entices the exactionist I am to set it right. And so I drive through Pennsylvania, Maryland and the District of Columbia with Mozart on the stereo and nothing on my mind but what the music tells me until I dock at my hotel. The hotel clerk is slender, shy and Ethiopian. At dinner the headwaiter's from El Salvador and smiles when I say that my former classmate at college was his former president, Jose Napoleon Duarte. He seems less impressed than surprised but tells me that he admired Duarte. The second waiter's Turkish and smiles when I thank him in Turkish, which is the only Turkish phrase I know. But this is Washington where populations alter year by year depending on the party in power or coups or revolutions elsewhere. Crammed with transients on expense accounts, the hotel advertises exercise facilities, a concierge, valets and a floor authentically numbered thirteen. High definition television sets in every room feature thirty-seven channels plus selected sports in progress, current movies on demand and porn. My pipes stay packed in a leather pouch because the hotel is "smokeless." I'm offered all the comforts of home but home itself. But then I realize I never feel at home unless I'm home, and then not always. So I accept this temporary home away from home for what it is and watch the news that tells me what the weather is back home, where snow's pre-dicted, but not much. Four days later I'm back where I started. I hope the house has missed me, but it seems exactly the same. My neighbors are still the same neighbors I've had for more than thirty years. Four days of mail are waiting. Indians in South Dakota need my help. A bank in England claims I've won the rough equivalent of half a million dollars, but I must respond by yesterday. Someone whose name I do not recognize is wishing me a happy birthday, which actually was four months ago. The Republican Party needs me more than ever now although I'm a Democrat. Finally finished with the mail, I learn that letters, catalogues and magazines weigh heavily when hefted in abundance to a garbage can. Unpacking both my bags, I follow in reverse the steps I took to pack, then lug the hollow luggage to the basement and decide I need to eat. I find the milk is rank, the lettuce wilted and the cold cuts clammy. Settling for cheddar on a Ritz cracker, I sag into an easy chair that convinces me I'm back intact and overdue in fact for sleep with half a cracker in my hand.

When General George Patton celebrated his advance into Germany by urinating in the Rhine, and Paris — liberated — still could not contain itself, I studied trigonometry without a thought that I would be spending days in the future in passage through the Indies, Europe and Asia Minor. I had yet to learn why first loves only rarely stick and how so much of living depends on luck, both good and not so good. If history's the name for how we try to understand the past, I've had my fill of history. It leaves me locked in memory's jails where all I'm left to keep is what I never had for long. Better to let what's meant to pass just pass as seasons pass around this house I temporarily call mine within this temporarily ongoing world. But just when I decide to try to walk away from history, some poet, at a most untemporary moment, stuns it to a stop with lines that stay as contemporary as the sky.

*J*erzy Kosinski was unquestionably the most interesting and intriguing man I ever met. Mute for a time as a child and shielded with his family from the Nazis by Polish Catholics because he was a Jew, he not only learned to speak but earned many degrees from European and American universities and, of course, became the novelist he was. Escaping the Nazi purge in Europe (later memorialized in his novel *The Painted Bird*), he ended in the United States. Over the years he became internationally known through his fiction. His novel *Being There* was made into a film (largely because Peter Sellers badgered Kosinski long enough for him to option the novel to Hollywood, even going to the extent of having his — Sellers' — stationery embossed with the name of Chauncey Gardiner, the novel's main character). A later novel, *Steps*, received a national award. Kosinski was well known in Hollywood and similar circles. He even was persuaded by Warren Beatty to take a small role in Beatty's film *Reds*. Kosinski was an inveterate traveller, an Icarian who jetted everywhere. While in Paris once, he received an invitation to attend a party in Los Angeles. Before boarding his flight to America, Kosinski was asked by an airport official for his final destination. When Kosinski said it was Paris, the official reminded him that he was already in Paris. Kosinski explained that he was going to be in Los Angeles for only one day and was returning to Paris. Ergo, his final destination was Paris. Kosinksi told me that this seemed too much for the French mind, and he missed the flight, and, because of a subsequent luggage problem, he never attended the party. In retrospect this was a blessing since the party in question was the very one where Sharon Tate and others were murdered by Manson and his fellow sadists. Kosinski also had his idiosyncrasies.

He ardently played polo, a sport not far removed from the sport of kings. He often accompanied police vice squads in New York on post-midnight raids. On one occasion, to prove a point about the aura given to uniforms by the general public, he had a Manhattan tailor design a uniform of a general from a fictitious country. He wore the uniform and was never stopped or questioned when he entered a restricted building without clearance or a theatrical performance without a ticket. In his last years he cultivated an interest in yoga, reaching such a level that he could "stand" upright in deep water without moving and not sink. In this vertical position, with only his head above water, he would cross his arms and become, as he said, "unsinkable." The whole exercise was even featured in a photographic essay in *Life* magazine. When I heard of Kosinski's suicide while I was driving home from work in the early nineties, I was so startled that I stopped the car. It seemed impossible for me to imagine that a man so "alive" could take his own life. Later I learned that he had various serious illnesses that left him totally depressed. When I wrote my condolences to his wife Kiki, she responded with a single sentence: "Your letter was a bridge to the rest of my life."

*A*mbassador Emeritus for years, he wore his usual gray suit with matching vest and a silk foulard indented at the knot. Ushered to his place of honor in a row reserved for dignitaries and their wives, he sat and waited. At ninety, he had earned the rites of tribute. Few of the guests recalled his final post in Canada or anything thereafter. The only reason they had come was to network and be "seen." The toastmaster, a last-minute fill-in, stumbled while reading a script he had just been given and not rehearsed at all. Twice he mispronounced the name of the ambassador. No one except the ambassador cared. His wife had told him once that it was far, far better to be totally forgotten than partially or incorrectly remembered. Childless and a recent widower, he knew the loneliness and vanity of honors never to be shared. With every word he heard, he felt he was being turned into a legend, that his life was becoming more posthumous than present. He wished he'd never come.

iles back I stopped to help a driver who had pulled along the berm. He waved me off, saying he'd only parked to rest, enjoy the scenery and smoke a slow cigar. Driving away, I, an Icarus of the road, faced again the yet undriven, dangerous miles. Road signs were fewer and fewer. The landscape was the same but seemed less welcoming and more remote. That left me with nothing else to do but steer and think. A few who'd come this way had said the miles would be lonely and become lonelier. Others preferred to clock the hours spent or miles driven from home as if the worth of traveling came down to numbers. Because all trips have to conclude, regardless, I laughed at their arithmetic. If some perceived this as a race, it seemed to everyone involved that no one was in a hurry to win. The final miles could not be clocked because the road divided into routes and by-roads headed for the same destination. I chose the one that seemingly chose me, just me. So on and on I drove, mile by mile, birthday after birthday.

It sprouted overnight with petals furled around a stem as upright as an exclamation point. And just like that the dreariness of Eastern Standard evenings vanished. For months each day was always yesterday, and yesterday meant ice and news of quakes and floods and war and memories of neighbors gone to graves. Because we missed the sun, the Caribbean beckoned, and some Icarians flew south for the winter. But those of us who stayed, although we rarely spoke and barely saw each other, earned the solidarity that stayers earn by staying. We shoveled snow from driveways, salted sidewalks and waited. And waited. Then all at once as if on purpose a crocus made me see the winter of our discontent as not a time of death but more like sleep. To end its sleep a single bloom appeared like something risen from the dead. Forget the parallels with Christ and Lazarus, although they're not irrelevant. I'm only saying what this meant to me. By staying put, I shared a resurrection that was somehow unforgettable because the waiting made me earn it.

"All books," one scholar said, "were people once." I think of that while thinning shelf after shelf of books I've read, re-read or just consulted down the years. With every book I'm letting go, I feel the jealousy of loss. I've known book owners with the souls of bankers. They accrue, accrue, accrue but rarely give or even lend. Handsomely ranked and bound on shelves, their books just rot untouched for years behind their spines and leather bindings. But who's enriched by leaving them unshared? From what I'm winnowing to lose, I hope new owners will discover why Vauvenargues claimed, "The thought of death deceives us, for it makes us forget to live." Or learn why Adonis would say, "He never burned; he never returned, this Icarus." Or savor Churchill's casual dismissal of paths that never crossed because his flight was cancelled, "Thus Herr Hitler was denied his opportunity of meeting me." Or relish Pope Roncalli's comment to reporters over Cardinal Ottaviani's rant against the Vatican Council, "If he is telling the truth, we should listen." Packing my books for readers I will never know, I realize that all we have is what we eventually can give away. The banker in me disagrees. What else explains why every book I grip is like a final handshake that I hold and hold until — begrudgingly — I let it go?

*A*re squirrels by nature never by a fraction fat or ever less than totally alert? Just look at them. With tails aloft they dart instead of run. To prove they can, they scale an oak-trunk to the topmost branch before they leap toward another branch or possibly a roof and rarely miss. Once I saw a squirrel misjudge his leap and land undaunted on all fours after falling thirty feet. I thought the shock might teach him to forego trapezing for a while. Instead the Icarus in him took over. He re-climbed, re-gauged, re-leaped and landed on a gutter spout as if the fall had never happened. He strutted off, his paw-steps herky-jerky as Marcel Marceau in perfect pantomime. This made me think of puppet soldiers powered by a switch to march like dolts or actual soldiers drilling on command — unshouldering rifles, clicking heels and cranking up salutes to metronomic and robotic cadences. The squirrels in all their perfect quirkiness make that and so much else appear unnatural and forced and false. It seems a minor point, but squirrels have proved this true for centuries with absolute indifference.

One bride at her wedding chomped on loud bubble gum while flouncing down the aisle. At another the groom and groomsmen wore white tuxedos with yellow ties and yellow sneakers. At a third the bride dallied for an hour outside the church because she wanted to be sure. At a fourth the groom, having passed out twice, was married seated and dizzy but determined. At a fifth the bride displayed a tattoo of the date on the back of her neck. And there were two who took each other for better or worse while skydiving down to Texas. Another two exchanged self-written vows with sign language side by side in divers' apparatus underwater. Just say that these are a few examples of how people in different ways prepare for a major step they've decided to take. Icarus was probably no different when he decided to marry the sky. What was on his mind just before he took off?

To be Prometheus is who we are when we are utterly ourselves — foresightful, daring, on the side of man. Sparked by the fire of God within us, we then see and say the truth as we know and feel it, or, perhaps, as it knows and feels us. We stand up not only for ourselves but for our kind. We see the present and, more to the point, where the present is heading. We are heat and light at the same time, and we want nothing else but to stay that way even though we know that sooner or later the world seems destined to bring everything down to the past tense of prose, to reduce the mysterious to reason, to postmortem life even as it is being lived. To all such inclinations Prometheans, like Icarians, are opposed. They are the avant-garde. They are where the cutting edge is sharpest, where life and poetry are synonymous, where attention is given to what happens as it is happening. They leave to Epimetheans those truths that have the dead strength of sandbags, and they bequeath to them as well the cold infallibility of retrospection and hindsight, which is thought in a state of rigor mortis. They are impatient with the seeming sanity and correctness of aftertalk. They are anxious to show the way, which must be found anew every day and which is a different way for every human being. Prometheus, the forethinker, has the courage of that vision and quest. Epimetheus, the afterthinker, is always in arrears. Forethinking as he goes, Prometheus lives as if each breath is his first and last, as indeed it is. To be Prometheus, therefore, is simply to be.

Blake occurs to me, Blake of the engravings. I see his cosmic nudes furled in fire. It is not the conflagrating fire that burns everything to ashes but a resurrecting fire that is almost like a nimbus glorifying the lives it is enfolding. The enhancement is apparent if you imagine a man against a series of backgrounds. First, a wall. Then, a cloudless morning sky. Then, a mountain. Finally, a waterfall of fire. Which one is more dramatic? Why? Perhaps it has something to do with light and danger. Light, because the fire leaves nothing unseen since it leaves nothing in darkness. It is brothered to lightning, to poetry, to the sun itself. It compels us to see just as a poetry stuns us into noticing what we saw but never knew we saw. It jolts us into seeing as lightning jolts us into seeing what it for just an instant illuminates. It mimics the sun, which by its very shining creates each slant and surface of a town that was hiding in the darkness all the time, waiting for light to discover it. And the danger that is also part of the nature of fire alerts us to its potentialities. It is power in reserve, fury in reserve. Blake put the fire of light and danger into his engravings. The memory of that fire is like an electrical field, keeping whatever it haloes forever from being inert, enhancing it in ways that are far beyond its own power to enhance itself.

*T*hink of fire as a tool. Tamed and focused to our purposes, fire is precisely that. It forges, melts, smelts, binds, bends, seams, steams, staunches and stills. It is actually the father and mother of all tools, since almost every tool in its most perfected form is in some way fire-fashioned. And like the fathering and mothering fire that begot and bore them, all tools wait to be used, and they realize their final beauty in use. I think of my hammer waiting for me on its side like a good dog. My hand knows its feel and heft even before I lift it to sink a nail. The sinking of a nail has a satisfaction of its own. My only way of describing its truth is to compare it to the sound of a pitched ball being hit by a willow bat. There is truth in that sound — in both sounds. That same kind of truth is in the beauty of tools, and it is as fundamental and unsubstitutable as fire or herbs. One cannot improve upon them. The focused fire of a blowtorch (I love the word) can turn metal into silver or amber honey, soften and lull it into shapes that exist only in the mind of the maker, fuse and forge simultaneously. This point of focused heat is where things are made to happen, and the maker is always and only man. Whether it is the controlled fire of a torch or the equally controlled fire in the maker's eyes, which, when trained on something with full and undeviating attention, is like the sun itself beamed into a tight, hot dot through a magnifying glass, it is the gift of Prometheus that is commemorated.

*L*ightning is a slap in the face, hard, unexpected. It is a simultaneous start and finish. It's over when it begins, but what it does in the bright instant of its life is bring the world up short. It flashes panoramas to a standstill. It is God's fire, and some people still call blessed the spot where lightning has struck. For Arabs the word for that is *baraka*. The fugue of lightning and thunder is as precise as Bach. First, the jagged line of lightning progressing instantly downward like a crack or suture in the sky. It is not a zigzag. It looks almost like a white skyriver heading for the earth, its destination uncertain, its tributaries feeding into it like minor vessels into an artery. Then, a pause like a breath being taken and held. Then, the skyburst and skyboom of thunder, which always begins at its loudest point and works gradually down and back to silence again. It is not unlike the yawn-deep bark of a lion. Lightning is like a crack of a whip. It tames us into creatures we actually are when we hear it. But there is another kind of lightning that remains in the clouds. On steaming summer nights you can look up and see illuminations in the clouds coupled with rumblings as if from thousands of caissons or howitzers being wheeled into position. In fact, the entire phenomenon is military. It is as if the burst of slashing fire and the accompanying drum-rolls were part of a sound and light show dedicated to Mars. The cloud-lightning resembles flashes from cannons on distant battlefields, and the thunder is a cannon-sound tumbling reluctantly downward to total silence before the next salvo.

ike man, a fire must breathe to live. When smothered, fires die. When fanned or bellowed, they thrive. Fire is thus an element within an element. It breathes to live. It lives to breathe. No wonder we apply to it the same qualities we ascribe to human beings. Like fire, we can be extinguished by suffocation. Like fire, we are unpredictably capable of erupting into furies that will burn on until they burn out and cannot be easily if ever controlled. Like fire, we are both creative and destructive — creatively destructive, destructively creative. Like fire, we are existential; we define ourselves as we go. Like fire, we can multiply ourselves. Like fire, we ascend. Like fire, we fall. Sensing this, Rimbaud claimed that poets must be thieves of fire, thieves of life itself. Like those who are able to catch lightning in a bottle, the thieves of fire must be able to steal life and somehow breathe it into their poems so that the poems continue to burn long after the poet's death, continue to share with those who experience the poem something of the light and warmth of the person who wrote it.

All those who are conversant with the myth of the phoenix know that it touches on the mystery of destruction and resurrection. The phoenix burns to ash. A new phoenix arises from the ash of the burnt phoenix. Poets at the time of Elizabeth and earlier saw in the story of the phoenix a very rubric of sexual love. By dying into one another, the lovers emerged as different selves, renewed selves. The instant of mutual release was not an expression of power or an act of cruelty but of self-extinction, of redemptive self-extinction. The very pleasure and joy of their satisfaction took what they each were at that instant and destroyed it so that, spent and fulfilled, they could discover and become another self that their lovemaking had created. It was not a mere conjunction of organs that the Elizabethans and their predecessors were talking about but a fusion of passion with passion into a single flower of eros. It was the fire of obliteration followed by a transfiguration. Although a promise of pleasure attracts us to lovemaking, it is more than the aftermath of pleasure that we reap. By such loving we can somehow be released from the tyranny of self in the most private of senses, which can be in some ways an imprisonment, and be a partner in a new freedom . . . one flesh, one fire, one new life from a fusion of two.

How dependent upon light we are. Keep us in utter darkness for hours or days, and we immediately show the effects of it. We scowl. We frown. We squint. We seem drained. We are like those coal or diamond miners who spend day after day in mile-deep shafts where the only light is the wee candlepower of their helmet beams. To the Egyptians of old, light was life itself, and they worshipped the sun as its source. Ditto the Mayans. Night was a synonym for death, and every nightfall was a deathfall as well. Gaslight or candlelight or a single wick burning on the oily surface of a glass of water was for centuries man's bleak attempt to mimic the sun in its absence. Until Edison. Edison is really the Prometheus of our time. It was Edison who electrified our century with a filament, a glowing gossamer that burned on in incandescence within a clear or frosted slur of glass no thicker than the shell of an egg. Through that invention we have illuminated houses, ships, aircraft, created flashlights, searchlights, floodlights (what would theatrical effects be without light?), lights that burn underwater, tinted lights, oven lights, lights that wait to say hello each time we open the door of a refrigerator, headlights, fog lights, courtesy lights, lights for interrogators, night lights, strobe lights, and every other flavor of light to prove that we continue to be Egyptians and Mayans after all.

orethinking is the mark of the visionary, and visionaries eventually express themselves in something they make. If they are poets, they help us see something whose truth is beyond denial or forgetting. If they are inventors, they make something that others may use and which would probably have never come into existence if they had not invented it. What is the proper reward for the poet or the inventor but wonder? Wonder and a form of unfocused gratitude. It is almost impossible not to be in awe of those whose inventions are inextricably wedded to happiness or downright necessity. Who invented ink? Who thus permitted man to create memory on a sheet of paper? Who gave every human being indelibility at the tip of a pen point? Who invented ice cream? Who invented the polka? Who invented the happy food known as cookies? Who invented kites and all the other toys that do not teach destruction? Who cannot help but praise those who make music, who create songs that become everybody's songs, who inhale the air around us and sing it back as anthems?

*W*ho first said that sexual passion was like fire? No matter. Let's go with the simile. If we are at times aflame with passion so understood, what could be more sensible than to focus and express it, to find words for our body-song? How honestly and beautifully the Sanskrit and Greek poets did it. But in our Jansenized culture — our Western skittishness vis-à-vis sexual love — we do not express our passion as readily as we repress or suppress or pervert it. The result is that it often emerges in such inhuman forms as cruelty or mere forcefulness. When we are out of harmony with our natures on this score, we move not toward the expression of our passion in words or song or coitus but in alternatives that move away from harmony toward cacophony — the cacophony of anger, conflict, and, in the final climax, war. In this regard, one social critic wrote pithily, "The modern equivalent of festivals is war." Why is there this distrust of sexual desire? The same distrust does not apply as strongly to our other desires. We live in times when our desire for things (or for people considered as things) is constantly stimulated and encouraged. We are confronted daily with a veritable pornography of stimuli through advertising and other sources to transform our desire for things into possession, which is the commercial equivalent of sexual climax. This has led some of our critics to say, with some truth, that we Americans love things and use people rather than love people and use things. As long as our sexual desires are held in such subliminal suspicion, there seems to be no way to extricate ourselves from this dilemma.

In the dark, nothing has color. Everything assumes the uncolor we associate with shadow. For the Greeks, dying meant moving into the shades, into the world of uncolor, into all that was the antithesis of the spectrum of life. In full light the rainbow that is life itself manifests itself without distortion. What tastes pear has the special green-yellow taste of pear. The black of Indian hair shines and speaks to us as polished ebony. The color of bananas is banana. Asphalt darkens with rain until the road becomes two roads — the road in sunlight and the road as painted by water into a darker version of itself. There is the brightness of lakewater at dawn, a different brightness of lakewater at noon, and a different brightness of lakewater at sunset. Yet it is the same lakewater or rather the same, different lakewater at each of these times. Only the light changes, and that change changes everything, just as a wheel spinning is actually three wheels — the wheel spun at full speed, the wheel spinning slowly to a stop, the wheel stopped. The French Impressionists understood. They remain the painters of light and of what light is able to do to color, shape, nearness and distance. All the great painters had the same love affair with light whether it was the slant light of the south of France or the clear light of Greece or the inimitable direct light of the sun or any of its man-made incandescent or torchlike imitations. When Picasso saw Francisco Goya's *Execution of the Rebels: 1808*, he saw it with the eye of a fellow painter. True, he acknowledged the obviousness of the Christ-like victim in the line of the about-to-be-executed, and he saw the synonymity and anonymity of the faceless soldiers. He saw all that. But what was the center of the painting for him? The fallen lantern and the wake of light that the lantern beamed across the whole scene.

I am thinking of the game that everyone plays when someone asks someone else to shut his eyelids for a moment and then open them. It could be a preface to a surprise, an event, a change of scene. For an instant in this circumstance someone places himself voluntarily in a darkness created by his self-seamed eyelids. He is certainly not asleep. He is fully awake, and his eyes want very much to see. They want that more than anything. They do not enjoy the darkness. Confronted by the interiors of eyelids that momentarily exclude the world that wants and waits to be seen so that it can re-exist in our perception of it, the eyes burn with the urge for sight, but all they see is a kind of pink and gray vagueness where something like a bent thread seems to be moving from left to right again and again and again. It has appeared before, this bent thread, when the eyes were eyelid-shuttered against noon. The pink and gray had been a steadier red at that time, but the same bent thread had ticked across that red sky, unhurriedly and even tantalizingly, knowing perhaps that a blink could vanquish it. But the time of waiting in this suspenseful but voluntary darkness passes slowly, slow as pain-time, slow as the clock of desire when it is not permitted to strike, slow as the evening of widows who sail the dark, deep seas of grief, slow even as the dawns of desperate fishermen who must wait for the weather to clear so that they can live. One hour, two hours. One day, two days. One year, two years. One century, two centuries, three centuries . . . At last comes the "open sesame" when the locks of the will are sprung, and the eyelids part to admit the world of light and every object that light defines just by being light, and the person who was absent from this world for the eternity of a minute is made a citizen of it again, and he feels that burst of joy that discovery and discovery alone can give him.

*S*mall as a wren (no, smaller), he navigates the inner branches of a bramble as deftly as the wind. He does it just to do it. Suddenly what has to be his mate appears. Perching coyly on a limb, she lets him tire of his bramble foolishness until he stops and joins her in an aerial duet that ends on grass. They chirp and hop, and then they mate, not merely to be satisfied but momentarily complete. That done, they wing away and leave me to recall how playfully they danced in flight before their *pas de deux* aground. It's always true that birds are nakedly themselves. I see it in the tick-tock tilts of the heads of robins and jays in a hunt for worms. They pose, pause, peck, pull up and swallow. The hens of the wild turkey investigate the turf with their beaks. This seems to be all that they do. The cock, on the other hand, parades like the king he assumes he is and fans his feathers as he struts and scans the world with total condescension. Aground, these creatures share what groundlings share. They eat and flit (fly + sit?) and mate and age. But when they fly they leave a grounded life for what the sky makes possible — a glide that fools the laws of gravity, a swerve and dive that orchestrates the will and whims of the wind, in fact a poem — a poem in itself that prose like this can only talk about.

Our ship was ocean-worthy, and we sailed on time. The storms that were predicted overtook us as predicted. Worse than the storms were the long and ominous calms. They made us think catastrophes were coming, but they never came. We blamed such nightmares on our fears, and so, like everyone, we lived two lives — one that we feared would happen, and one that happened regardless. We said whatever we could not expect was all we should expect, and that became the way we thought until we reached the shoals. We knew that no one would survive since no one ever had, but when and how the end would come was hidden from us. All that we knew for sure was where we were and where we saw the ship was heading. That's where we are right now. The preceding could be a parable of sorts. But any trip, regardless of destination, symbolic or otherwise, has moments of boredom en route. In fact, boredom is often the stepchild of travel, no matter what the mode. At some point in his flight Icarus must have tired of looking down at the monotony of the surface of the Mediterranean Sea before he thought of heading for the sun to relieve the boredom.

What is called a Promethean sun is now a stanza of horizontals vanishing westward to Virginia and from Virginia westward still to the Mississippi and from the Mississippi to Nevada and the Palisades and from there across the Pacific and over the volcanic isles and then over Japan, China, and the Asia that is called Minor and then arching over the puzzle-pieces of Europe and then in a leap across the Atlantic to this curve of the Potomac where we are watching horizontals of color that are a blend of peach and rose and orange with a hint of canary at the base and another hint of indigo at the apogee. We talk about light — the light that love or insight brings to the eyes, the light at the end of a burrow of darkness where one friend with a lantern is waiting for us like a sentry on permanent post, the light that is the hope that is life's last word against surrender. Word? What is each spoken word but a lightsome breath we draw in and sound back to the world, and what is the word we write or publish but a code of marks that come fully alive in the light of print? But we are not now thinking of such but only of the westward and westering banners of the spectrum fading as our very minutes together are fading toward midnight and the daily Easter that is morning. We seem content with that, as if the darkness that is already happening is the pause between light and light. Call that the sleep of Prometheus. All people, even lovers, share it in separation before the dawn once again shall unite them.

In the high office of his stovepipe hat he moved like some gaunt woodsmen garbed for Sabbaths of discomfort. His arms dangled. Most things he seemed to know without remembering — the rhythm of the King James psalms and Paul Bunyan's boney English. All that his second mother, Sarah Johnston, taught him stayed with him and stayed him like a spine that never buckled. Wounded by the girl he perhaps should and would have married (now long since dead and buried in Illinois), he spoke and wrote with a tall sadness all his life . . . sad long before slavery made war its only answer. He broke his sadness with jokes the way the verbs of jumping trout break up for the better a lake's calm noun. At almost six and a half feet, he stood a head taller than his cabinet and later his generals. In photographs he looked unhappily at peace but quietly assured. In spectacles he looked intelligently assured. Happy with Anne Rutledge, he might have stayed on in Illinois as A. Lincoln, Lawyer. But something of the buried love of one dead woman readied him for less, for more. It woke the poetry he wrote aloud in Gettysburg that still defines us as a people. It opened him to a world and words that being untragically happy would have kept reserved within him, as a man keeps secret what he loves the most because the saying of it is beyond him. With all that happiness lost but unforgotten, Lincoln faced the worst of any nation's inner ills with something of the equanimity of a man to whom the worst has already happened. In such a circumstance, he saw clearly, saw through, saw steadily through. Not for fame did he see, since he had long before learned that fame meant only that thousands or millions he would never know would some day recognize his face and name. Nor was his vision something he could share. A citizen of the outer limits of pain,

Lincoln lived in the uninterrupted solitude of visionaries. For what then did he live? For the country, of course. For the nation that persisted in the poetry of his hope for it long after Booth and his bullet turned that hope into us.

Vowers I revere because they swear forthrightly on their very souls what fear or circumstance could easily incline them to foreswear. I speak of oaths where all the hurts and thirsts and hopes of living blend and focus — vows that even death cannot undo. What are they? There are, admittedly, vows and vows — some said before a cross, some sworn on sacred books or on a memory or on a mother's grave, some felt within the blood and never brought to words. Vows like these last are those that define the ultimate morality of which we are capable. Such vows come into being when we learn that we cannot betray what we live by even when the opportunity to do so presents itself. It is not merely what we won't or shouldn't do. It's what we can't do. The mere doing is so beyond us that we would be undone by it; it would convulse and contradict our very natures. At that instant we are (God help us) who we truly are, or rather who we cannot help but be — naked in our very natures and sworn to be so because we cannot be otherwise without destroying ourselves in the process. It comes back to what Aristotle said of us — "As a man acts, so he is." Not as a man talks or thinks or even imagines himself to be, but as he acts.

To write is to bleed. To want to write is to know you have been wounded, and since wounds bleed, you prepare yourself for the bleeding. You know you are bleeding, and you continue to bleed until the bleeding stops. It is your very life that is coming out of you, and it has a will of its own. You cannot wish it otherwise. You cannot order your wound to heal. You cannot pretend that you are not wounded. Like blood, your writing is often a transfusion — a passing on of life to life. It is not just a matter of words and punctuation marks and ink and paper. It is your life that is being passed on. That is why those who think that writing is merely a craft are so far from the mark. It is as fundamental and mysterious a force as blood. It is unstoppable once it starts, and it obeys only its own laws.

It flapped across the road and headed south — a veritable stork, I swear, in storkless Pennsylvania. For parallels, imagine polar bears in the Bahamas, Christmas Eve in June or anything that has no business being where it is. It took priority at once. It changed a neighborhood we thought we knew into a neighborhood-with-stork. But then what less can be expected from the unexpected? Storks, tornadoes, lightning, Auden's "Musee de Beaux Arts" or a murdered savior risen from the dead — they make us look around with different eyes, they shock, they re-arrange the world.

think of the Chevrolet that missed me by an inch — the topmost step I overlooked just before I caught myself in midstep — the swim that I survived by luck in the Atlantic. Dumb luck and close calls are not the only silencers. Anything at all can leave me mute: a scream, a crash, a shot, the stench of skunk smell in the wind or the sight of Manolete's shirt with all the bloodstains yellowing to shadow after fifty summers. Each one reduces me to silence or blind utterance where yesterday means nothing, and tomorrow less. My life comes down to now as all I have. That much. That little. The feeling's even darker when it comes in dreams. Asleep, I seem to be yearning for light as keenly as an underwater swimmer burns to surface and breathe. Waking, I ask myself what day it is? I'm not awake enough to answer nor asleep enough to dream. The house keeps talking to itself like an old man with no one else to talk to but himself. The tang on my tongue of last night's coffee lingers like a fault. So does the aftertaste of dinner — was it pork chops or tilapia? Surfacing slowly from sleep, my body works and waits for me to realize what's happening. My eyes interrogate each corner of the room. All this is not as simple as insomnia. It's more like time without a name — half-day, half-night, half-true, half-not. I keep remembering Ron Padgett's, "The day will come when your life will seem to have lasted an instant." The house I worked to buy for someone else some day to buy becomes a parable of sorts. Housed in my temporary skin, I'm nothing but a tenant myself. This leaves me stalled between a past that seems as brief as a remembered day and the short or lengthy but uncertain dream I've yet to live.

*W*hen you're ill or injured, it's almost predictable that you feel the dark closing in on you. Your horizons shrink. Your plans evaporate. Your expectations are not what they were yesterday. You are married to your illness or your hurt. You are pulled to take an almost possessive interest in it, and it wants to have all your attention so that it will be dominant over you, so that it will set new limits to your life. If you accede, you become your cough. You become your infection. You become your fractured bone, and you become as solicitously sensitive about it as someone in the grip of some vice or indulgence becomes solicitous and privately possessive about that. You become like a miser with his coins, an alcoholic with his bourbon, an envier with his private itch to hate everything that is good (an Elizabethan interpretation of envy, and not a bad one at that) simply because it is not his. It seems to me that sicknesses and injuries, perhaps like death itself, are to be faced and intelligently hated (as one hates deliberate ignorance, for instance) so that they do not assume dominance. A life intimidated at every moment by death becomes a study in fear, hesitation, and hopelessness so that the intimidated person is in fact already under the control of that intimidation. It is no different with sicknesses or injury. If the intimidations of one or the other begin to dominate, the person is thereafter owned by his infirmity or disability. The only answer is a kind of knowledgeable scorn, if such an attitude is possible. And that scorn or rebuke is actually life's response to whatever it perceives as its enemy.

In military units in combat or attack situations, there is a single soldier or a small group of soldiers designated as the point. It is their mission to scout ahead of the main body so as to detect and hopefully avoid ambushes or unexpected confrontations with the enemy. They are often called the advance guard and resemble the avant-garde in literary or cultural circumstances — those who are out ahead of the mainstream, who are looking for the best directions, and whose decisions influence and often dictate the course that the mainstream will follow. These people are Icarians and Prometheans in the real sense. They need the courage that the loneliness of their mission requires them to have. They know that life is a matter of motion and that such motion cannot be left to chance without risking destruction or disorder or waste. But their courage is secondary to their judgment. They must be astute forethinkers in order to determine which direction is the best without knowing that in advance, since such foreknowledge, from their and any human perspective, is beyond them. They rely on their own discriminations, their own instincts, their own very sense of things, their sense of history, and, finally, on the luck or faith that is ultimately the soul of whatever decision they make.

*S*omeone who believed in history once said that the past is all we have. I have no mortal quarrel with this. The past is what is behind whatever prompts us to preserve it in the present in universities, in libraries, in archives, in museums, in scrapbooks. It is behind what can make us the very ward of our memories. It is also what gifts us with continuity. For this reason most people feel nothing but sympathy for those who have had their memories destroyed or marred by strokes or for those who suffer from amnesia. But what if the past is simply regarded as a burden, and memory a kind of curse? This would mean that stroke victims and amnesiacs are somehow spared the burden or effort of remembering. For them the past is a shut door, and life is always and only what is right now happening. They face the present and where the present is going. I realize that this is not a popular view and that I myself truly hope that I will never be picked to prove it in my own experience. After all, to people who have lost much in their lives, memory is possibly their only treasure. And there is the unavoidable truth that knowing what is behind you helps you know where you are and where you are heading. And it is equally true that much but not all of our knowledge is what we have at one time learned. But the natural emphasis on the present in our living cannot be ignored. Children live without effort in that state. The time is always now, which is also and always the time of thought, breath, fire.

We read backdated updates and believe that yesterday's today. This mimics in reverse the way we live. Each time we speak of now, it's then. Intent on saying what we're saying even as we say it, we've already said it. As for the time being, whatever's happening becomes what's happened even while it's happening. It leaves us living always in arrears. We try to understand what's never understandable in passing and finally give up. By then it's much too late for anything but resignation. We're not disturbed to find our plans disrupted since we have no plans. We wander like the lost from now to now — from here to here. To distract myself I spin a globe of the world. The hemispheres and oceans blur. The twirled and miniature world reminds me of the earth as photographed from space — a speck among the galaxies. But where in all these revolutions hides the legacy of Julius Caesar, Pippin the Short, Confucius, Cicero and Shakespeare at their peaks or, less importantly, the "horizontals" of Versailles? They blur as if to prove we're fated to persist as fading recollections only. What miracle can put a stop to this? The spindled globe I'm spinning numbs me with its pantomime of how the earth has always answered: one spin per day, twelve months of daily spins per year. Each time I spin, I'm spun myself. Spun, I just keep spinning. I think of Henri Cartier-Bresson who said, "Life is just once — forever." He aimed his lens to mint a moment he believed decisive into memory. That was all . . . one man with a Leica. In white and black he froze the once and only-ness that others see too late or never. He meant each shot to be read, not merely seen, as we would read a map, a poem or the face and form of someone loved. His photos match in nothing but their differences: a boy with bottles, lovers at the Bateau Mouche, a woman being fitted by another woman with a wig, Malraux in painful concentration, Sylvia Beach in her bookshop with Shakespeare's portrait on a wall behind her, Arthur Miller somber in Connecticut. Models he never posed nor ever cropped a shot to make it any other than a miracle as first and final as a birth.

nless there's something to touch, my fingertips just wait. The same applies to ears, nostrils and tongue that need some hint of sound, scent or taste so they can hear, smell and savor. Eyes have a will of their own. Before each morning's reveille they search for sightings in the dark while to the other four "th'objects must come home." Eyes speak the language of eyes to other eyes. And they remember everything from freshly ironed and folded shirts in a drawer to the way Clemente's bearing at bat or afield owed more to demeanor than to prowess and practice or to Margaret Mead's precise description of pornography as sex separated from personality. Whether distracted or diseased, eyes become nobler as regrets or losses. Either way, mortality enhances what they were, are or can be. Even as metaphors their aim is clarity. What's worse than being eyed to scorn? Or dearer than saying to your dearest, "You are my eyes"? Or better than being a sight for sore eyes or the apple of one?

Assuming a mother's role for a young expectant wife whose own mother could not be there, my wife attended the birth. She saw not only a firstborn son but the birth of a mother his birth created. Today that son is over thirty and a father himself with two brothers and a sister. The mother who could not come is gone but present even more in absence. Three decades later to the day my wife and the mother now of four remember and embrace. Without a word they share what spans a generation. Bonded by a night of labor that begot two births at once, they hold each other's hands while sitting side by side in a tryst of touch and silence.

It climbed and rested in a birch before a state trooper numbed it with a tranquilizing shot. It dropped to the ground through a tangle of branches. Black bears had never scavenged in suburbia before. This one had entered through a kitchen door left open while the owners slept. He helped himself to bowls of sugar and barbecue bones in the garbage. Television news featured shots of the bear, still tranquilized but caged, being trucked to a zoo. It seemed an isolated incident (and was), but still it showed we're never far from wildness, without or within. A bear in a kitchen scoffs at postal zones and property lines. It's all just space to him. His only guides are instinct and a nose for food. In the same neighborhood that night a thief was caught red-handed pilfering a shopper's Lexus. Leaving nothing to chance, a trooper tased, cuffed and drove him stunned to jail. For malice, blame the thief. For hunger, blame the bear. Leaving morality aside, the outcomes were the same.

If fiction is an alternate reality, it's not confined to books and films. I see it in ads inviting me to spend the golden years of my retirement in a condo on the gulf, security included. I see it when I spot a uniform because all uniforms create an alternate reality. I see it in television's merry-go-round of fare segmented to the limit of attention spans. I see it in face-lifts, transplants, tucks, cosmetics, dentures and dyes. I see it in fashion, styles, stardom, honors and the bogus royalty of wealth. I see it when ideas spoil into isms. I see it in the very dream that fictioneers call life. Who knows if life's finale is a second birth or a dated death? They both suggest an alternate reality, a fiction.

*O*n Goya's *Cinco de Mayo* the soldiers are one times seven. They rhyme in rank, their rifles aimed, their right cheeks crunched against the riflestocks. Those chosen to be murdered rhyme with no one but themselves. One stares with arms uplifted like a crucifix of everlasting protest. Others cower or scream or look to God. The rest just cringe beside each other in a sprawl. Before the firing squad, they seem disordered as humanity itself. It seems too much like melodrama to be true, but bullets were fired, and people were slain. Yet not a soul but Goya thought it worth the time to paint what faded in the faces of the dying when the faceless soldiers shot.

Call it the natural state of everything — a rack-full of neckties waiting to be worn, a Guernsey about to calf, the way each moment's poised until whatever's now becomes whatever's next. You see it in squirrels aground before they jump to circumnavigate a tree — in sprinters crouching at their blocks and ultra-ready for the gun — in shelves of hats awaiting heads. It leaves you asking which is truer — the time that is or a time to come. Somehow the answer's in the asking. And so you wonder whether now is all you have or if there's more. If now is all, then living's not a preface but an end. If not, what then? In time you'll know, but now there's just the asking.

*T*ranslating the October tint of Japanese maples into language is a challenge. Red is wrong. Burgundy's too dark. Maroon lacks luster. Still, the sheen of each leaf needs an adjective to modify a noun's brightness to define it. Tempted to try, I leave the morning paper folded and unread. What difference does it make if I'm not currently abreast of the world's bad news? Since news is over long before it reaches me as news, why should I fret? I'll focus on the here and now until I choose the right word to match the color of leaves in slow passage from scarlet and russet to … Ruby? Vermillion?

Regarding love as unpredictable as luck, health or the weather, he opted to pursue esteem. He chose whatever brought him money and acclaim. It filled the void. It made him famous overnight but cast him in a role. People addressed the role, not him. He tried disparaging the role with humor. The role prevailed. It locked him in its total armor. Shelved in his ocean-side home were plaques, citations, statuettes, framed photographs, medallions on gold mounts and keys to multiple cities. After he retired, he hoped that aging would return him to himself. And so it did. Predictably he came to see renown for what it was. He auctioned his awards and gave the proceeds to his hired help. Predictably he wanted someone to share himself with — someone to care for — someone who cared. Often he awakened after midnight and for hours stared at utter darkness that stayed unmerciful as agony and silent.

*D*elivered each dawn, it waits as thrown for him to retrieve it. Some days it feels too heavy to carry. He blames the weight on a surplus of bad news along with stock reports, obituaries, comic strips and ads for new cars. Later, with the news no longer new, he folds the paper as it came and throws it in the trash. But never is it unretrieved or left unread while he sips every morning's coffee. It's all that links him to the turning and returning world. It helps him feel included.

Imprisoned by a frame, the sad nudes of Modigliani seem the sadder. Likewise Picasso's acrobats, El Greco's saints and all the dancers of Degas...Why does each masterpiece remind me of a field no longer flowing into other fields but suddenly interred behind a fence? I've had my fill of frames, including stamps or coins commemorating Lincoln, Roosevelt, Mae West or Liberace — horizons snapped in focus through an aperture and fossilized in color — portraits in cameos embossed on gravestones in Provence. Designed to honor or immortalize, they come across as posthumous and spare as funeral announcements limned in black. In different ways they say we're here to have but not to hold, that what was once unframeable cannot stay mute as silence in a box but waits to be remembered like a wound too deep and inaccessible to heal.

*L*ast week when I surprised her on the lawn, she played the prima donna, bolting away like a beautiful, ungainly girl attempting to flee in heels. Last night she roamed with her faun, nosing for fallen apples or simply nosing. Freed from his usual woods, the faun cavorted like a colt before he tired and behaved himself. This morning the doe and faun returned with a stag. Although they knew I watched, they posed with statuesque aplomb and munched. Elsewhere, lions could be chomping a zebra carcass to its ribs. Or polar bears devouring baby seals in a single swallow. Everywhere the curse of hunger — viciously destructive and insatiable, but not, compared to us, malicious....

wo plump robins are back from Sea Island, Tallahassee, Tampa, wherever. They circle and land with absolute precision. For them this is the first day of the first March of the first year of their remembered world. While we keep numbering away our years, they live without counting. Pheasants and turkeys strut with their harems in tow. Monogamous cardinals arrive. The male's vermillion trumps the female's khaki camouflage. So much for ornithology. The male parades and preens. The female blends with the scenery. On high a swarm of wrens surrounds an unsuspecting hawk and slowly forces it aground. What other species perches, chirps, mates, hatches, navigates without collision, dives, sings and dies on the wing? They never seem to rest. Even when nesting they appear in motion. "The worse my drawings were, the more beautiful did the originals appear." That's Audobon the artist talking, not Audubon the ornithologist. His paintings of American birds seem flawlessly complete, but never quite. As renderings, the paintings do as much as paintings can. What's missing is the mystery of flight.

It's bound to happen. Clouds will flock and darken. Grass will flatten in winds that whip the limbs and leaves of trees in one direction. Thunder will drum its tympanies, and lightning slash its exclamation points to make a noon of night. All this is overture. The storm, if it comes at all, could be as soft as Irish rain or undeterrable as fusillades or salvos aimed at everything. Later there might be outages, floods, uprooted timber and ruptured power lines or nothing more than a steady drizzle or a false advisory. What makes me think of Shakespeare's "Blow, wind, and crack your cheeks…" or "Mountains are in labor for the birth of a ridiculous mouse"? It's Lear in all his lunacy or Horace at his most sarcastic, but the fanfare stays the same.

Everything about him was precise: the centered knot of his necktie, the shoes burnished to a gleam, his crew-cut almost militarily exact. Though Peruvian by birth, he spoke with no accent and seemed completely at home in American. He said the wrist surgery would be done in one visit without anesthetic but would require two weeks to heal. "Your wife...you cannot lift any weights in that period." After a pause I said, "My wife died in July." The Peruvian in him came to life. He gave me the half-hug of an *abrazo* and said slowly and softly, "She will be with you forever."

The forced glee she gushes when hugging voter after voter will survive in selfie after selfie. Backed by a Las Vegas billionaire whose money talks, the nominee from Florida smiles on cue like merchandise. A loner who bankrolls himself and answers to nobody else hallucinates out loud and brings down the house. Reborn in the Lord, a lawyers proclaims he speaks for Jesus, who tells him everything to say. Someone asks, "Is this democracy, or is this vaudeville?" It's vaudeville.

It took his son's son to say what everyone felt for this older city cop, who kept his aches and sorrows to himself. One grandson in his twenties lifted us in those few minutes past the ritual, the flowers and the talk to something truer than them all. Considering the pain we knew he felt, the effort was heroic. Policemen later cleared the cemetery road where sailors waited at attention with a flag tri-folded to accentuate the stars. And no one saw as inappropriate the honor of bequeathing to the casket just before it closed a U. S. Navy cap and three robusto cigars.

In each of four sons, one daughter and their children, he survives. And in the eyes of all the widows of the friends who died ahead of him and in the mower he drove enthroned to tame the lawn. And in the taste and aftertaste of grape leaves stuffed and cooked with no more lemon than enough. And in the quiet pistols cleaned and locked away. And in the cars, the cars, the cars — each one a fraction larger than the rest because big cars were made for bigger men. And in the tears he could not stop the night his father died. And in the baseballs Jason threw for strikes in flat Ohio. Or when Dolores says his name again, and then again. Or why his sister, my wife, knows he's gone but not away because our son has something of his stance and walk. Or how he left us suddenly while watching television after midnight by himself — the channel changer in his hand but useless.

Whatever wants to say itself through you is busy being born. It takes no less than all your attention — all your time. You know from other labors you have suffered in the past that all the pangs of bearing fade upon delivery. But now you struggle with the paradox of finding words so say what cannot be said directly, if at all. It could take hours, weeks or years. Or just a second. Nothing's predictable except your will to say it right. For just that long you're more than someone clocking out a lifetime, more than history. Each thing you see becomes the first and last and only version of itself. It wants to be both once and always in the words you hope will keep from passing what you know will pass. You can't look backward or ahead until whatever you have tried to see and say and save as unpredictably as possible is seen and said and saved.

*H*er credentials impress: doctorate and baccalaureate from Denver, Master's from Notre Dame, pianist of concert quality, distinctions in academia, politics and business, an oil tanker named Condoleezza, Secretary of State et alia in the Bush regency, post-administration honors, degrees, citations, speeches priced at thirty, fifty or two hundred and seventy thousand per speech. Her defense of torture never disappeared, nor did Israel's invasion of Lebanon sanctioned by her, the Decider-in-Chief and Lord Anthony Blair, but by all others condemned. Results? More than one thousand civilians killed, a million displaced, runways and highways cratered, water and power plants bombed as well as a coastal refinery whose oil-slick fouled beaches in Lebanon, Syria, Turkey, Greece and Cyprus for years. Leaflets were dropped south of Beirut, warning residents to leave their homes on hour before they were bombed. Families near Hamra were strafed in flight, then strafed when they returned to find an old grandfather in the rubble. Too crippled to move and unreachable, he'd starved to death. East of Saida, two million cluster bombs waited in the hills for children to find them… Meanwhile she met with her invading allies in Tel Aviv, proclaimed the birth of a new Middle East and prepared to fly to Beirut. Ignoring protocol, the President of Lebanon told her not to land.

It came to you as sounds conspiring in a special way an inch or two before you fell asleep. Too tired to write, you said it had to wait until you woke. By morning it was gone, and you had other things to do. Remembering without regret what never came to be is not your strongest suit. You tell yourself to think of something else, but that just makes it worse. Even now the ache of having lost what could have turned out well unsettles you. It calls to mind the boxed gift you lost before you chose to open it. Some say that writing out your disappointment helps to compensate. You disagree. The lost poem keeps its distance like a woman scorned and unforgiving.

Surely you have seen his head — eyes fore and aft to see what's coming and what's past at the same time. Impossible, of course. What's yet to come is always unpredictable. and what's past is plagued by contradicting judgments. If Janus is the god of foresight and hindsight, he stands apart from life as we live it — minute by minute when the stakes are high. Facing the charging lions of our hungers or the quiet snakes of fear, we have no time for anything but instinct. Later, if we survive, we slowly look around or finally within, not straight ahead or back. Where else is there to look?

His aviator's eyes come with the calling. Like someone taking aim, he squints at gauges, runways and horizons. He thinks in minutes instead of miles. From Pittsburgh to DuBois — eighteen minutes. To Meadville — thirty minutes. His world's a mix of flight paths, time and altitude. Present at his solo, I watched him taxi, take off, circle and land three times to qualify. Because it's no small thing to do something well enough to have it stamped official, he smiled a totally earned smile. Ahead now would be cross-country or transoceanic flights in Boeing 757s or higher. His motto would be "the sky's the limit."

*allen or felled, they litter forests like so much random timber. Those broken by rot, storms, age or lightning lie where they crashed, their branches spiking turf. Uprooted, the naked roots resemble ganglia desperate for air, for life. Those axed or buzz-sawed down by loggers leave only the gravestones of their amputated trunks. To gauge the age of trees by counting circles in their table-top stumps I leave to finalists. What matters most to me is what precedes finality: the early sepia of Japanese maples softening to amber, a chorus-line of spruces trimmed and topped like hussies, the leaflessness of oaks in snow. Even hardwoods chosen for lumber have an afterlife. Cut down and rafted by river to sawmills, the logs return transformed as barns, domestic architecture, furniture, burls for carvers and whittlers or, finally, kindling. I side with the stayers that last through bluster and balm until it's time. I see them then as sentries numb from standing stiffly at attention in the sun for days before they topple back or forward from attention at attention.

Many say that walls of houses are only for protection. Others say that walls without pictures are like pages without print. Framed on walls, pictures give walls a different presence just as painting a white wall blue creates a totally new wall. Defining things according to their purposes yields nothing but the minimum. Describing what they make us feel can change us just as music listened to alone can change us. Poets would understand and prove it true with poem after poem. And so would actors who assume the lives of different characters so perfectly on stage that audiences forget they're acting. So too would those onlookers who see pictures on walls and hear them speaking silently aloud like print from open pages.

NEXT seemed an utterly American name for a store, as in next customer, next order, next day. In most European stores, there is no next. The current customer comes first, and everyone else can wait or leave. Oriented more to the passing present than a present to come, Europeans stay abreast of time while we plan and anticipate as if what's next is all that matters. The store called NEXT markets watches and clocks where time is tallied to the split second. That's understandable for sales. For life what's next can be surprising or even final. Before the ultimate, Saroyan's last words say all that each of us might say, "What's next?"

I'd never paddled alone in a canoe. Daring myself to try, I paid for a rental, ensconced myself in the stern and pushed away from shore. Before stroking, I packed and lighted my pipe, surveyed the lake for other rowers and paddled to the lake's center like a pro. For just that long I freed myself from front-page slaughters, the posed America of televised hypes and scams, the on-line frauds that pass for higher education and poets who behave and speak like poets. Buoyant as a bar of soap, the canoe rolled, stroke by stroke, until it rolled too far and over. All social headaches vanished with me in the water. When I surfaced, the canoe had righted itself. I saw people on shore pointing at me. I swam toward them, pushing the canoe ahead until it grounded. "Are you all right?" one stranger asked. I nodded and managed a grin before I boarded the canoe and stroked with utter textbook balance back. With every stroke I wondered what he must have thought of me in my soaked shirt and shorts while I was still holding in my mouth a pipe filled to the brim with lake water.

Problems attack. You have to be ready whether you're ready or not. They overwhelm like love. The blindfolded baby with arrow and bow can hit whatever he's not aiming at. There's no defense. Surprise or infiltration will surprise and infiltrate. Targeted, expect no option but reaction. Delay like anybody cornered by dilemmas. Pause before you choose. Weigh all the consequences. Yesterday's fool could be tomorrow's hero. Results cannot be known in advance. Regret is just as likely as assurance.

It's mid-May. The flowers are slowly becoming flowers. The grass is as green as possible. I've come outside to read Dower's *The Violent American Century*. He claims that an American First Strike would target 295 cities in Russia, killing 115 million people. He footnotes that a single megaton bomb from the American arsenal is four thousand times as powerful as the Hiroshima bomb. The numbers repeat themselves incessantly as drummers drumming. Meanwhile, azaleas are living up to their promise. A single finch is pecking for seeds in a feeder, and the lawn is more than leaves of grass. Flowers, birds and lawns have different agendas. They're always busily busy being what they live to do until.... There is not so much as a hint of drumming. One earth, two worlds.

*O*ff comes the old roof, shingle by shingle. Pried-up nails litter the yard beside yestersummer's shingles. That done, the roofers open carton after carton of new shingles, which make the old shingles look even older. After hours of re-fitting and pounding, the new roof waits for sun, snow or rain in the total readiness of being roof. A woman being fitted with a chosen hat appears the same. After much tilting and turning to get the hat just right, she'll view herself and see she looks surer and newer. It's the hat that does it.

On the nudist (nudest) beach in St.Tropez, two couples, naked as God's originals, stood and chatted like any foursome. Both men were smoking Gitanes. Their wives in identical sunglasses listened and laughed. Were they in clothes, their tete-a-tete would be no different in Paris... Both sexes were volleyballing next to them. The behinds of the players resembled rear faces, not two the same. Sprawling to return a serve, they rose with sand sweated to their chests, breasts and totally public privates — circumcised, uncircumcised or shaven. Mildly pregnant, a sub kept score ... Seventy yards away a lone cameraman focused his Leica for close-ups that were there for the seeing up close. Everybody on the beach had chosen to be stripped of modesty and shame in favor of utter frankness. If naked meant unclothed, and nude meant being naked permissibly in places like beaches or life classes, the results were similar. Everything exposed. Nothing revealed.

It's sentry-time. Framed pictures keep the walls from being boring. The house is talking to itself in French. Outside a car passes as if reluctant to be a lone car moving after midnight. Everything seems irrelevant as yesterday's weather. This time is not the time the clocks are telling — tock by tick. It's more like moments spent recovering from agony or loss, or writing by hand a letter that must be written, or letting the mind become as open as possible to prove that nothing's better than to be — simply to be.

"Came we quite naked hence," so wrote one scrivener, "and go we quite naked thence." And I agree. I think of Icarus whose legacy is what he did with nothing but his wings. I think as well of nomads and Apaches who thought that those who travel light travel best. And I agree. To those who claim that enough is never quite enough, the sailor in us knows from sailing that accumulation is a fault. It leaves us baling as we go to keep from being drowned by sheer abundance. Afterward we learn it's liberating to be free of junk, of memory's relentless follies and regrets, of wants that weigh us down, of information by the ton, of all the draining wounds of guilt. Beyond the minimal, what more is needed to survive? Compare barefooted distance runners from Ababa with any helmet-hooded soldier armed for murder. Who is the freer man? It seems just common sense to rid ourselves of anything averse to riddance long before what's unforeseeable and sudden rids us of ourselves and everything we say is ours — rids us of it all forever.

Other Works by Samuel Hazo

POETRY

They Rule the World
And the Time Is
Like a Man Gone Mad
The Song of the Horse
A Flight to Elsewhere
Just Once
As They Sail
The Holy Surprise of Right Now
The Past Won't Stay Behind You
Silence Spoken Here
Nightwords
The Color of Reluctance
Thank a Bored Angel
To Paris
Quartered
Once For the Last Bandit
Twelve Poems
Blood Rights
My Sons in God
Listen with the Eye
The Quiet Wars
Discovery

FICTION

The Time Remaining
This Part of the World
Stills
The Wanton Summer Air
The Very Fall of the Sun
Inscripts

CRITICISM

Smithereened Apart: A Critique of Hart Crane

ESSAYS

Outspokenly Yours
The Stroke of a Pen
The Power of Less
The Pittsburgh That Stays Within You
The Rest is Prose
Spying for God
The Autobiographers of Everybody

PLAYS

Tell It to the Marines
Watching Fire, Watching Rain
Mano a Mano: A Flamenco Drama (The Life of Manolete)
Feather
Solos
Until I'm Not Here Anymore

The author of books of poetry, fiction, essays and plays, Samuel Hazo is the founder and director of the International Poetry Forum in Pittsburgh, Pennsylvania. He is also McAnulty Distinguished Professor of English Emeritus at Duquesne University, where he taught for forty-three years. From 1950 until 1957 he served in the United States Marine Corps, completing his tour as a captain. He earned his Bachelor of Arts degree magna cum laude from the University of Notre Dame, a Master of Arts degree from Duquesne University and his doctorate from the University of Pittsburgh. Some of his previous works are *They Rule the World* and *Like a Man Gone Mad* (Poetry), *The Time Remaining* and *This Part of the World* (Fiction), *Feather*, *Mano a Mano* and *Watching Fire, Watching Rain* (Drama), *The Stroke of a Pen* (Essays) and *The Pittsburgh That Stays Within You* (Memoir). His translations include Denis de Rougemont's *The Growl of Deeper Waters*, Nadia Tueni's *Lebanon: Twenty Poems for One Love* and Adonis' *The Pages of Day and Night*. One recent book of poems, *Just Once*, received the Maurice English Poetry Award in 2003. He has been awarded twelve honorary doctorates. He was honored with the Griffin Award for Creative Writing from the University of Notre Dame, his alma mater, and was chosen to receive his tenth honorary doctorate from the university in 2008. A National Book Award Finalist, he was named Pennsylvania's first State Poet by Governor Robert Casey in 1993, and he served until 2003.

www.ingramcontent.com/pod-product-compliance
Lightning Source LLC
Chambersburg PA
CBHW032100080426
42733CB00006B/361